ARTEM KUDELIA PHD

Integrative Therapy

Personal Transformation Guide

This book is not intended to substitute for professional medical or psychological advice or treatment if necessary. It is recommended that you consult the appropriate specialist if you require medical, psychological, or any other professional assistance or treatment.

If you are experiencing severe symptoms of a serious mental or physical health condition, the advice provided in this book may not be suitable or sufficient for you. If you have not already done so, it is strongly advised that you seek the guidance and collaboration of an experienced mental health professional or medical practitioner.

If your symptoms or issues worsen while reading this book, it is important to stop reading immediately and seek help from a qualified healthcare professional.

The author, publishers, and any subsequent distributors of this work are not responsible for any errors, assumptions, or interpretations made while utilizing this information. Readers have the sole responsibility of understanding and making use of this information.

First edition

This book was professionally typeset on Reedsy.
Find out more at reedsy.com

Contents

Acknowledgments

I would like to express my gratitude to my psychology and psychotherapy teachers, who have opened the path and laid a solid foundation of knowledge. Furthermore, I extend my immense appreciation to patients, colleagues, friends, and all individuals who directly or indirectly contributed to the writing of this book.

BONUS: Get Your Free Resources Now

I'm excited to share a **free eBook** and **exclusive access** to **psychological resources** with you. To get started, scan the QR code or visit psychemaster.com/integrative-therapy

What You'll Get:

- **Free eBook**: Explore advanced psychotherapeutic techniques and approaches that complement the insights.
- **Interactive Learning**: Engage with exercises and quizzes to solidify your understanding of complex theories.
- **Latest Research**: Stay updated with the most recent findings in the field of psychotherapy and integrative therapy approaches.
- **Continuous Support**: Get consistent tips, strategies, and motivation to assist you in staying focused and excelling in your studies and practice.

Maximize your understanding of psychotherapy!

Integrative Vector

Many contemporary therapy approaches are related to different vectors, combining some of them. Often, two, three, or sometimes four vectors are involved. However, in my opinion, only a few are able to combine all or almost all vectors to some extent, forming an integrative presupposition in the system for adopting various methods and elegantly combining them.

The initial division into pure psychoanalysis, behaviorism, humanistic therapy, and transpersonal therapy is gradually becoming a thing of the past as different therapists find their way of combining different methods, discovering that the correct combinations can yield excellent results in working with patients. However, we believe that the integrative style of psychotherapy implies that the philosophical foundation of the method itself is based on the concepts of acceptance, borrowing, and coexistence with other methods.

In a sense, the integrative style is not an assortment of different styles but rather a **metastyle** or a model of models that can simultaneously incorporate unique therapeutic methods.

Neuro-Linguistic Programming

Neuro-Linguistic Programming (NLP) has become the primary representative of the integrative vector in psychotherapy. It was created in the early 1970s by Richard Bandler and John Grinder. Richard Bandler was a psychology student who regularly conducted gestalt therapy sessions at the university, while John Grinder was a linguistics professor who once visited Bandler's group and became interested in what he was doing with his patients.

Grinder attempted to create a specific "map" of linguistic patterns used by Bandler during his work. They then joined forces and started working together on what later became known as the meta-model.

John Grinder

They began studying the works of renowned therapists in order to capture the linguistic structure of what they do and the correct questions they usually ask patients to evoke insight and catharsis, thereby manifesting the "magic" of psychotherapy. They focused their attention on five therapists.

Richard Bandler

These were Frederick Perls, the creator of Gestalt psychotherapy; Milton Erickson, the author of non-directive hypnotic suggestion; Virginia Satir, the creator of family therapy; Frank Farrelly, the creator of provocative therapy; and Moshe Feldenkrais, the creator of the Feldenkrais Method. They also actively collaborated with psychologist, ethnologist, and anthropologist Gregory Bateson, who played a significant role as their mentor and consultant. It is worth mentioning that the works of American anthropologist Carlos Castaneda, who studied the shamanic traditions of Mexican Indians, significantly influenced the emergence of early NLP.

Map of the World

Initially, Grinder and Bandler were intrigued by the linguistic structure used by therapists. They based their assumptions on the idea proposed by linguist Korzybski in 1933, that "the map is not the territory," meaning our perception of the world is not the actual world, and the language we use is a way to operate with the "map" of the world. Bandler and Grinder introduced the notion that our language shapes our map of reality, and this shaping occurs through three fundamental processes.

1. **Generalization:** The process by which several different experiences are grouped together in consciousness into one category or, based on a new experience, a separate category can be formed. For example, a child gets an electric shock. Their consciousness generalizes the experience and perceives all other electrical outlets as potentially dangerous and capable of causing pain. We do not need to recheck each socket for the danger of its impact. Experiencing or witnessing it once is enough.

2. **Deletion:** When we acquire a specific experience, we only describe a part of it with our language. We use this part in the process of social communication, conveying

it to others. The other part of our perception that is not formulated in words is either omitted and does not become conscious at all, or it is gradually suppressed into the realm of the unconscious. In the context of verbal communication, for instance, the phrase "I'm glad to see you" can have various meanings for a person. The underlying meanings may be hidden behind this phrase. We do not request the specifics that lie behind it; we mostly operate with the "label" rather than the actual object.

3. **Distortion:** A significant portion of the map is formed through the analogization of one experiential block with another, representing something as a metaphor for something else. In ancient cultures, many such analogies were used to compare human qualities with the behavior of different animals. The process of analogization is closely related to the construction of myths and ancient beliefs. By blending different experiential categories together, we gain more opportunities to use them qualitatively in our lives. At the physiological level, the process of distortion can be explained by the emergence of multiple connections between neurons in the brain. It is important to remember that the intelligence of a living being depends much more on the quantity of connections between brain neurons than on their actual number. The process of distortion is closely linked to the process of personal creativity, allowing individuals to create something new that was not previously represented in their perception.

Based on their understanding of the three fundamental processes of reality mapping, Bandler and Grinder began formulating specific clarifying questions that a psychotherapist can ask a patient to help them fully grasp the deep structure of their experience. We typically use surface structure in verbalization and thinking.

Examples of surface-level experiences can be phrases like "She doesn't love me," "They don't understand me," or "The world is a war." Within each phrase, various meanings can be embedded, significantly differing in the understanding of different individuals. From a set of different clarifying questions that allow for the realization of the deep structure of experience, the first model in NLP emerges—the Meta Model.

The first two collaborative literary works by Bandler and Grinder are dedicated to this model. These two volumes are "The Structure of Magic," in which they extensively explain how this model can be applied in the context of therapeutic work.

Metamodel

Let's explore how different questions can be categorized according to the three processes of reality mapping. We will provide examples of correspondences highlighted by Michael Hall.

Distortions

1. **Nominalization** refers to words that cannot be perceived through the representational systems of perception. They cannot be seen, heard, or physically felt. However, they always carry specific meanings. The key ideas embedded in nominalizations may be identical for everyone, but the secondary ideas and details of the first and second can vary significantly.
   Examples of such words include "love," "equality," "brotherhood," "collaboration," "understanding," "harmony," and "freedom," among others. Examining the meaning of these words without interpreting the specifics can lead to a cognitive error.
   Clarifying questions to eliminate the cognitive error of nominalization are as follows:
   "What exactly do you mean by the term 'freedom'?"
   "What specific actions do you perform when expressing

your love?"
"By what criteria do you determine that what is happening between you is friendship?"

2. **Mind-reading** involves certain statement phrases that imply the presence of a cognitive process, emotion, or state in the subject of discussion without mentioning the sensory criteria through which this information became part of conscious awareness.
   Examples include "I see that you are a good person," "I think you understand me," and "I feel that we will work well together."
   Clarifying questions can be as follows:
   "What exactly do you see that allows you to consider me a good person?"
   "Based on what thoughts did you assume that I understood you?"
   "Which specific sensations enable you to understand that I am a good person?"

3. **Cause-effect linkage** is a linguistic construction that implies the mention of two events where one is perceived as the consequence of the other. However, the experience that could provide an understanding of why these events are causally linked remains unexplored.
   Examples include "If you eat little, you won't grow," "If you don't listen to me, you'll remain foolish." "If you show off, you won't get candy."
   Clarifying questions can be as follows:
   "Based on what specific information did you come to the conclusion that if I don't eat, I won't grow?"

"How did you understand that I would remain foolish if I didn't listen to you?"
"What served as the basis for your belief that if I show off, I won't get candy?"

4. **Complex equivalence** occurs when one nominalization is equated to another. The equation can be perceived literally or metaphorically.
   Examples include "love is war," "freedom is harmony," and "life is a stream."
   Clarifying questions can be as follows:
   "What exactly allows you to equate love and war?"
   "Based on what criteria do you compare freedom and harmony?"
   "What specific experiences in your life allow you to compare life and a stream?"

5. **Presupposition** refers to a statement that contains a secondary implied meaning not explicitly expressed in the message text. There are 29 different types of presuppositions. Here are some examples:
   Phrase: "Next time we will do better."
   Presupposition: "There have been previous times."
   Phrase: "He bought the fifth car."
   Presupposition: "Four have already been bought before."
   Phrase: "Do you realize that you understand me?"
   Presupposition: "You understand me."
   Clarifying phrases can be as follows:
   "Do you mean that there were previous times?"
   "Do you mean to say that four cars were already bought before this one?"

"Do you mean that I already understand you?"

Generalizations

1. **Universal quantifier:** In this case, we are working with predicates that generalize certain experiences. These words include "all," "always," "no one," "never," "nobody," "nowhere," "no way," and so on.
   Example usage of this pattern: "All people are the same," "It always happens like this," "Nobody wants to understand me," and so on.
   Unpacking questions:
   "Name those people whom you consider to be the same."
   "Can we consider these people as 'all'?"
   "What do you mean when you say it always happens?"
   "Does it happen every day, every minute, every second, or are there time limitations?"
   "Who exactly doesn't want to understand you? List them."
   "Is there a possibility that somewhere there are people who can understand you?"

2. **Modal Operator of Necessity:** The use of phrases like "I cannot" and "I must." *Examples*: "I cannot afford to do it today," "I must stay where I am."
   Unpacking questions:
   "What exactly prevents you from doing it today?"
   "Is there a possibility to overcome these factors?"
   "What exactly makes you stay where you are?"
   "Have you ever tried not staying where you are?"

3. **Lost Performative:** A phrase that does not specify the

author who created the message or the source from which it was taken.
Examples: "Men should provide for women," "Women should cook, clean, and give birth to children," "Children are the flowers of life," "Take care of yourself."
Unpacking questions:
"Who is the author of this message?"
"Where was the information taken from?"

Omissions

1. **Indefinite Noun**: Inanimate objects without specifying additional information.
   Examples: "I returned to the house," "They bought a car," "Set an alarm clock," "In this case, it's better to take a trombone."
   Unpacking questions:
   "Which specific house did you return to?"
   "Which car did they buy?"
   "Which alarm clock should I set?"
   "Which specific trombone is better for me to take?"

2. **Indefinite Verb**: Verbs without specifying the details and specifics of the action being performed.
   Examples: "They run," "They perform on stage," "He falls asleep," "Someone shouts."
   Unpacking questions:
   "How exactly do they run?"
   "How exactly do they perform on stage?"
   "How exactly does he fall asleep?"
   "How exactly does someone shout?"

3. **Incorrect Comparison**: A sentence that presents a comparison without specifying the basis for comparison or the criteria used for evaluation.
   Examples: "They are better than everyone else," "These students are smarter than the others," "He possesses greater strength."
   Unpacking questions:
   "In what specific way are they better than everyone else?"
   "How did you determine that these students are smarter than the others?"
   "How did you determine that he possesses greater strength?"
   "How exactly was this strength measured?"

4. **Lost Referential Index**: In this case, words such as "someone," "some people," "they," "doctors," "psychologists," "engineers," "tourists," "volunteers," and so on are used in speech and thought.
   Examples: "Someone is waiting for you," "Some people are already at the starting line," "Doctors know a lot about medications."
   Unpacking questions:
   "Who specifically is waiting for me?"
   "Who specifically is already at the starting line?"
   "Which specific doctors know a lot about medications?"

Michael Hall's Metamodel

Michael Hall expanded upon the Grinder and Bandler model by introducing additional cognitive distortions inherent in human thinking and speech.

1. **Identification:** This metamodel pattern clarifies any unspecified identification used in speech. In the alternative meta-model, we will consider two specific forms of the identification pattern. In this case, we view the model element as the most abstract form.
   Examples: "liberal," "party-goer," or "judoka."
   Unpacking: "What specific meaning do you attribute to the word 'liberal'?"

2. **Statistical Terms:** This pattern unpacks phrases that rely on statistical data. Formally, this pattern is a variation of the lost referential index in the classic NLP metamodel.
   Examples: "English scientists have proven that... ." "Scientific research confirms the validity of our hypotheses."
   Unpacking: "Which specific English scientists are you referring to?"

3. **Over / Under - Defined Terms:** This pattern reveals excessive descriptions of an object or process, creating a specific representation of the discussed object, or simply inadequate descriptions that do not provide a complete understanding of the subject matter.
   Example of excessive description: "I really wanted to do what I had been dreaming about." "Given the conditions of my life, I was not able to do it." "So, I decided to take a step that could change my life."
   Unpacking: "Please specify more clearly: what specifically motivated you and what action did you take?"
   Example of inadequate description: "This largely determined the course of events."
   Unpacking: "Which specific course of events did it determine?"

4. **False verbal dichotomies:** Occur when there is a direct denial of the influence of one process or phenomenon on another.
   Example: "My financial well-being has nothing to do with the political situation in the country."
   Unpacking: "Based on what criteria did you come to the conclusion that your financial well-being has nothing to do with the political situation in the country?"

5. **"Either-Or" Words:** This pattern presents an ultimatum, offering only two possible choices while ignoring other potentially viable options.
   Example: "Either you listen to me or you leave."
   Unpacking: "What other possible courses of action exist for me in this situation?" "What are the reasons for this

strict limitation of choice—either one or the other?"

6. **Pseudowords:** In this case, words with vague and sometimes absurd semantics are used, which can significantly differ in meaning when used by different people.
   Example: "You're crazy."
   Unpacking: "What exactly do you mean when you say I'm crazy?"

7. **Multilevel Statements**: This pattern involves a phrase in which the logical level that should determine the meaning of the message is not specified.
   Example: "How can you allow yourself to do this?"
   Unpacking: "Could you clarify the meaning you attribute to the question?" "What answer or action would you like to receive in response?"

8. **Personalizations:** This pattern occurs when a person takes someone else's action or emotional reaction personally without considering real sensory criteria. Actions are often interpreted negatively, making this cognitive error predominantly characteristic of paranoid personalities.
   Example: "You don't look at me during our conversation, so you must be plotting something against me."
   Unpacking: "Based on what reliable sensory information do you form your judgment?"

9. **Metaphors:** The use of analogies and metaphors in communication does not fully reveal the true meaning of the message but rather diverts from it and often misleads the

interlocutor regarding the actual content of the message.
Example: "He grew up like a weed by the roadside."
Unpacking: "What do you mean when you say he grew up like a weed by the roadside? Does this metaphor objectively describe the process of his growth?"

Initially, Bandler and Grinder did not think that their work could take a separate direction in psychotherapy. In their work "The Structure of Magic," they comment that the model they describe can be perceived as auxiliary to any form of therapeutic work, and they do not claim to form a separate direction in psychotherapy. But time proved otherwise. They continued studying the works of various therapists and began forming notions about the structure of other therapeutic mechanisms. Different people gathered around them, actively participating in their research and studying the structure of personal experience and expertise.

A short time later, when the seminars conducted by Bandler and Grinder became quite popular and when they started teaching not only the meta-model but also new models, there arose a need to somehow name what they were doing. There is an amusing legend about how the name NLP itself emerged. Whether it is true or fiction is hard to judge, but it is not of substantial importance. Before one seminar, Richard Bandler, John Grinder, and their associate Frank Pucelik were sitting in a car, contemplating what to call their field of activity. They actively discussed the topic for some time but could not reach a consensus. Soon, one of them noticed a stack of books lying in the car. One was about neurology, another was about linguistics, and the third was about programming. The combination of these three key words gave the name to the method that is still known as neuro-linguistic programming.

Although NLP itself was formed in the context of modeling by well-known and successful psychotherapists, it was not essentially psychotherapy but was defined by its creators as the "science and art of modeling subjective human experience." That is, it could effectively apply to various spheres of human activity. It is precisely because of this that NLP has spread widely to other areas of human endeavor, such as politics, advertising, business communication, interpersonal communication, etc.

Formally, the meta-model was intended for correcting cognitive distortions that may occur in an individual's experience, and in this sense, the meta-model work closely resembled cognitive therapy by Aaron Beck and rational emotive therapy by Albert Ellis, although it had some differences. Due to the initial focus on cognitive correction, it can be said that the primary vector in which NLP developed was the cognitive vector.

Anchors

The next significant vector was the behavioral one. The creators of NLP borrowed the concept of acquiring a conditioned reflex from Ivan Pavlov. A similar term used by behaviorists, particularly John Watson and B.F. Skinner, was "operant conditioning." Both imply the ability to elicit an old response through a newly established stimulus.

For example, Pavlov did this with dogs by creating an association between food consumption and the activation of a light bulb in their physiological reactions. Later, when only the light bulb was presented to the dogs, the scientist observed the secretion of gastric juice. Or how Watson did it with the little boy Albert. He showed him a white rat, and when the boy laughed, the experimenter struck an iron gong behind his back to induce fear. After a certain number of repetitions, Albert began to display fear in response to the white rat.

In this case, we see the restructuring of a response, where the previous stimulus is replaced by a new one. Naturally, based on the works of Pavlov, Watson, and other scientists, therapeutic methods were developed. Behavioral therapy, which applies the restructuring of old responses to new ones through operant conditioning, became widely known in America. Most likely, it was from behavioral therapy that NLP borrowed the concept of "anchors."

Anchors can be of various types:

- **Natural anchors**: Imprinted in our physiology, they are reflexive. For example, it can be a reflex to pull your hand away when touching something hot.

- **Spontaneously created anchors:** For instance, when you were in the company of pleasant people and heard a new musical track, two stimuli became associated. After some time, when you hear that track again, the state of pleasant interaction you had previously experienced reappears in your consciousness.

- **Artificially created anchors:** In this case, states are intentionally linked. For example, when a patient experiences a resourceful state that needs to be anchored, the therapist touches a specific point on their shoulder and applies consistent pressure for 5–15 seconds. Then, when there is a need to reproduce the state, the therapist simply presses on the same point again to activate the desired state.

Types of anchors:

- **Visual anchors** can be external or internal. A typical example of an external visual anchor is a fixation on the image of a familiar person that evokes a stable positive reaction. The response to an internal image involves visualization. For instance, you imagine that there is a party awaiting you tomorrow, and pleasant sensations arise in your body.

- **Auditory tonal anchors** can be both external and internal. With an external anchor, you may hear a loud noise and experience anxiety. With an internal anchor, you create certain sounds yourself that change your state. For example, humming a children's song that puts you in a humorous mood. The effect of an auditory tonal anchor is directly related to the sound itself, not the literal semantic meanings that words and phrases may carry.

- **Auditory discrete anchors** elicit a response not to a simple sound but specifically to the semantics of a word or phrase. It can also be external or internal. With an external anchor, you may hear the phrase "Get up!" and automatically jump out of bed. With an internal anchor, your state changes when you articulate a specific semantic construction or simply do it solely on the level of thinking and inner dialogue.

- **Kinesthetic anchors** are activated when there is any touch on the body, such as stroking, a strike, or a push, etc. For example, if you experience anxiety and are slapped on the shoulder at that moment, a subsequent slap on the shoulder can trigger the anchored state of anxiety. Kinesthetic anchors can also include taste and olfactory stimuli.

- **Motor anchors** are activated through the repetition of specific motor dynamics or statics. For example, while in a specific posture, you experience a strong sensation. Later, when you assume the same posture again, the sensation

> returns. Similarly, the dynamic aspect can come into play. For instance, you memorize a particular sequence of movements, let's say a dance routine, in a fixed state. Then, when you repeat the sequence of movements, the anchored state returns.

These types of anchors are specifically used in brief therapy sessions to evoke positive changes in patients.

One of the classical techniques in NLP that utilizes anchoring is "collapsing anchors." In this technique, a negative state is associated with one anchor, which is then targeted for therapeutic work, while one to three positive statements are associated with another anchor to counterbalance the negative anchor.

The negative anchor is activated first, reestablishing the negative state, and while it persists, the positive anchor is activated. Both anchors are held simultaneously for a period of time, after which the negative anchor is released, followed by the positive anchor. This pattern is fundamental for working with kinesthetic anchors, although a similar anchoring method can be effectively applied to other representational modalities.

The downside of working with kinesthetic anchors is that direct physical contact with the patient or interlocutor is required, unless in a therapeutic context. In some cases, these physical touches may be somewhat inappropriate. It is important to consider this factor, especially when dealing with patients who belong to certain psychopathological profiles and may not be receptive to physical contact. Schizoid personalities serve as a striking example of such profiles.

In such cases, the use of visual and auditory anchoring may prove effective. For example, during a conversation with the patient, one can inquire about resourceful states in their life. While the patient comments on these states, subtle fixed gestures can be made with the hand or another body part, thereby creating a visual anchor for that particular state.

Later, when the conversation touches on sad topics, the visual anchor can be subtly reproduced to introduce the resourceful state into the negative context, thereby overriding it. Similarly, auditory anchoring can be employed by using rhythmic tapping on the table with fingers or an object instead of a hand gesture.

Changing Personal History

A highly intriguing therapeutic technique in NLP is the technique of altering personal history, which is rooted in psychoanalysis and hypnoanalysis. In this technique, the therapist guides the patient into the past to work through their traumatic experiences.

The classical approach utilizes anchor techniques for this purpose, although other methods of state change can also be employed. Initially, the therapist elicits the patient's concern or issue, such as the fear of public speaking. Then, step by step, the therapist assists the patient in traversing their personal timeline, identifying when this fear originated in their life. Gradually, they aim to reach the root cause of the fear, uncovering when it first emerged and under what circumstances, thus reviving it in the memory during the therapy session.

Subsequently, the therapist dissociates the patient from the current problem and inquires about three resourceful states that were lacking in all the contexts associated with the fear of public speaking. The patient determines the necessary states, and the therapist helps them locate instances of experiencing those states in their own life. These states are then anchored.

Moving forward, the therapist re-associates the patient with the earliest manifestation of the traumatic experience and activates the resource anchor. Finally, the patient gradually progresses along the timeline to the traumatic experience that has been recalled. In each subsequent negative experience, the positive anchor is also activated. Once the overlaying of negative states with positive ones is completed up to the present moment, an additional practice can be introduced.

The therapist asks the patient to shift into the future and imagine themselves speaking publicly. When the patient successfully recreates this future scenario, the therapist also activates the resource anchor, thus programming the anticipation of the experience yet to come. There are numerous variations of this technique, and its execution should be calibrated to suit the individual patient and their specific needs. A dry and mechanical execution may fail to yield comprehensive therapeutic results.

Submodalities

Working with submodalities is an intriguing practice in NLP. Submodalities represent the qualitative characteristics of the primary modalities of perception - visual, auditory, and kinesthetic.

Visual submodalities	Auditory submodalities	Kinesthetic submodalities
Brightness	Loudness	Intensity
Contrast	Tone	Temperature
Focus	Intonation	Pressure
Color image	Reverberation	Pain sensitivity
Black and white image	Echo	Location of occurrence
Image mobility	Mono/Stereo	Volume of sensations
Image static	Spatial sound positioning	Sensory differentiation
Spatial image position	Sound intensity	Direction of movement of sensations
Presence of frame on the image	Classification of sound source	Onset and decay rate
Direction of image movement	Sound quality	Diversity of sensations
Image movement speed	Sound refraction	Cyclicity of sensations

For example, a large, bright, moving image that is closely related to your possible future achievement is likely to evoke strong positive emotions. Meanwhile, a small, dull, static, and distant image will not evoke any emotional reactions.

Naturally, it has been discovered that we can instrumentally change one submodality of experience to another, thereby creating new emotional reactions and recoding existing or potentially possible experiences. The application of submodalities, like anchors, has a very wide range of applications in NLP and can be used in various contexts.

The simplest example of working with submodalities in practice is the direct transference of submodalities. For example, you recall an experience that evokes negative emotions and place the image of that memory to your left. Then you focus on the key submodalities that encode that image. Next, you recall an experience that consistently evokes positive emotional reactions. You place the image of that experience on the right side of your imaginary screen. This image is also analyzed to determine the predominant key submodalities. Once the main submodalities in the two images are identified, there is a sequential recoding of the negative image into a positive one, where the image itself does not change but its submodal code does. For example, if the positive image was in color and the negative one was black and white, we would transform the negative image into a color image. However, it should be understood that direct transference of resource submodalities is not always suitable for therapy. If we simply want to improve our relationship with someone, submodality recoding of their image into a more positive one may be appropriate. But if we are working with an image of an animal attacking the patient, it would be more appropriate to apply dissociating submodalities to the image, making it small, distant, and black and white.

A simple one-time change of submodalities in some cases will have a strong effect, while in others it will not. There is a concept that, in our experience, so-called critical submodalities can take place. When a critical submodality is activated, an experience that used to evoke a fixed emotional reaction undergoes a radical change in quality and starts producing a stable, different emotional reaction.

Each person may have their own personalized critical submodality, but an example can be provided. One of the best options, in my opinion, is the critical submodality of a bright flash. First, the patient is asked to recall a negative experience that consistently triggers a negative emotional response. Then they are asked to recall a bright light from a welding machine. After that, they are instructed to overlay the image of welding fire onto the image of the negative experience and hold it there for some time. If done correctly, the negative image seems to fade away, and when attempting to access the negative emotional experience, the patient experiences difficulties. Either the emotional intensity significantly decreases or disappears altogether.

The effect of using critical submodalities is often quite strong and stable.

Reframing

In the original NLP, two main types of verbal reframing were considered. The term "reframing" can be interpreted as "shifting into new frames," reforming, changing the frame, or transferring meaning from one frame to another. Primarily, it refers to frames of meaning. Initially, NLP founders identified two types of reframing: context reframing and content reframing.

Context Reframing

Context reframing involves transferring a specific behavior from one frame of meaning to another, where the meaning of that behavior changes significantly and can even become diametrically opposed to what was characteristic in the previous context. For example, behavior involving physical aggression on the street is potentially disapproved of. However, when placed in the context of a boxing ring, it can acquire positive and socially acceptable meanings.

Content Reframing

In content reframing, the context itself remains unchanged, but meanings are selected in such a way that the evaluative judgment of the behavior changes and becomes diametrically opposite. A typical example of content reframing could be the phrase, "He is not slow but rather thoughtful and unhurried."

Language Patterns by Robert Dilts

Robert Dilts extensively explores the topic of reframing in his book "Language Patterns." Essentially, Dilts' model is an enhanced and expanded version of the reframing model proposed by Grinder and Bandler. He identifies fourteen reframing patterns. Let's list each of them and briefly discuss their application.

1. **Intention:** The question is posed as to whether a certain behavior has any positive intention that can influence the process. An example of a positive intention could be the desire to attract attention through the manifestation of an illness.
   Example: "When he is sick, he receives enough attention."

2. **Redefinition:** In this case, a different definition is given to a behavior, process, or belief, thus radically changing the emotional reaction to it.
   Example: "He is not cowardly but rather a very cautious person."

3. **Consequence:** Attention is shifted to the positive consequences of a negative process or belief.

Example: "Even though you lost your bag, you clearly gained some vigilance."

4. **Separation:** In this case, attention is directed toward certain details of a negative process or belief. By focusing on them, the frame's meaning can change dramatically.
Example: "Even though you were late for work, you heard the song of such a beautiful bird."

5. **Unification:** The question is asked: "What larger logical element of the class to which the process or belief belongs can shift its qualitative perception?" In simplified terms, the question is: "If this is bad, what is good?"
Example: "Even though you were very scared during the parachute jump, you still went through with it."

6. **Analogy:** An analogy or metaphor is chosen that, on the one hand, suits the description of the process or belief, but on the other hand, qualitatively shifts its assigned meaning.
Example: "Hercules also cleaned the Augean stables" (to someone who is tired of cleaning a room).

7. **Frame resizing:** Temporal, quantitative, or qualitative characteristics of the process or belief are changed, creating new constructive meanings that differ from the original ones. For example, we take and expand the potential time frame based on which the negativity of an event ceases to be perceived as significant.
Example: "When you look at the current problem from the perspective of your entire life, you only see it as

experience."

8. **Alternative outcome:** It is indicated that there are other, different from the ones presented, possibilities for the development of a situation related to the process or belief. *Example*: "Sometimes being fired becomes a stimulus for a person to start their own successful business."

9. **Alternative outcome:** In the context of this reframing pattern, an alternative perspective on the process or belief is offered, one that is inherent to someone with an alternative worldview.
Example: "From a psychiatrist's point of view, you represent a very interesting case."

10. **Reality strategy:** The sequence in which a person experiences sensations in order to perceive the process or belief as negative is determined. Then, an alternative strategy is suggested.
Example: "Even though he looks terrible, his speech is so pleasant and warm!"

11. **Opposite example:** It is indicated that any exception confirms the rule. The result of the process or belief may be something diametrically opposed.

12. **Hierarchy of criteria:** Attention is focused on the existence of some other criterion related to the process or belief that can significantly alter its perception.
Example: "It's not about who wins or loses; it's about the game continuing."

13. **Self-application:** The question is posed: "Is it possible to logically apply the meaning of the process or belief to oneself?" Thus, a paradoxical logical process is created. *Example*: A patient says that he is very afraid. The therapist responds, "Okay, can your fear be scared?"

14. **Metaframe:** It is assumed that there are other beliefs or processes based on which the current belief or process can undergo significant semantic transformation. Formally, it all comes down to considering which belief holds a higher hierarchy, and attention is fixed on it.
Example: "Today he behaved terribly, but being truly best friends means accepting each other with all the pros and cons."

Six-Step Reframing

A well-known technique in NLP is "**Six-Step Reframing**." It aims to create a trance-like state in the patient, where the work primarily involves their unconscious mind.

The first step involves identifying the request that the therapist will work with. In the second step, an "analog signal" is established as a non-verbal communication system with the patient's unconscious mind. The patient's unconscious mind is directly asked to raise the index finger of their right hand if they want to answer "yes" and the index finger of their left hand if they want to answer "no." After this, the unconscious mind is asked if it wants to interact in any way at the moment, and if it responds "yes," the process moves to the third step.

The third step involves addressing the symptom that the therapeutic work will focus on. The symptom is asked whether it has a "positive intention." It is worth explaining and commenting on the fact that NLP presupposes that behind every symptom lies a positive intention. In other words, the manifestation of a symptom is simply a way of not knowing how to do something optimally. For example, a person who overworks and exhausts themselves at work, despite knowing that they are pushing their limits, is ignoring their body's signals. Once their unconscious mind "realizes" that the body won't get any rest, it forms a symptom that forces the person to stay at home, rest, and not work. The positive intention behind the symptom is fundamentally beneficial, and if a constructive outlet can be provided, the symptom itself can be eliminated. Often, in the third step, the part of the person's personality responsible for the symptom answers "yes" to the question related to the positive intention.

Following this, the process moves to the fourth step. In this step, the therapist addresses the creative part of the patient's personality and suggests creating three or more new ways of fulfilling the positive intention for the part of the personality responsible for the symptom and then transmitting these methods to it. If the creative part of the personality agrees to do this, the process moves to the fifth step, where the part of the personality responsible for the symptom is asked, "Are you willing to accept these methods if they are suitable?" If it agrees and accepts the new methods, the process moves to the sixth step, where a request is made to the entire unconscious mind of the patient to determine if there are any other parts of their personality that may hinder the implemented solutions. If the response is positive and such a part exists, a new cycle of the technique is applied from the third to the fifth steps. If everything is going well, the technique concludes.

There may be other additional steps in this practice. For example, upon completion, it is possible to express gratitude to the unconscious mind for its cooperation, thus demonstrating therapeutic courtesy. This technique has many nuances that are challenging to describe in detail due to the considerable variability of responses to the technique among different patients.

Rapport Building

One of the key background practices in NLP is the technique of rapport building during the process of psychotherapy, which Bandler and Grinder borrowed from their teacher, Milton Erickson. Although such a practice can also be found in the works of other psychotherapists, Erickson used this technique as one of the key elements in establishing rapport with his patients. Through rapport building, he was able to establish deep trust even with psychotic patients.

We explore Milton Erickson's work in more depth in the chapter dedicated to the hypnotic and provocative approach in psychotherapy.

Rapport building when working with patients can take various forms and include a multitude of nuances. Let's consider several types of rapport-building.

- **Breath mirroring:** During communication with an individual, it is important to synchronize one's breathing with theirs. The key criterion for successfully practicing this technique is maintaining a rhythm in the breath. People who breathe in a rhythm similar to ours are perceived as close and friendly individuals.

- **Posture mirroring:** Directly mimicking someone's posture in regular communication is not suitable for rapport building, as the patient may perceive it as literal parody on a conscious level, which can trigger resistance. However, partially mirroring posture by reflecting the main contours of body positions can have a positive influence on the communication process.

- **Gesture mirroring:** When mirroring gestures, it is not advisable to immediately start with a full replica of the interlocutor's movements. It is sufficient to replicate the general outlines of the gestures, as if tracing them, and it can also be beneficial to reproduce the repetition with a slight delay of 3–15 seconds to make the mirroring less noticeable to the interlocutor.

- **Speech pattern mirroring:** In this type of mirroring, tone of voice, intonation, volume, and timbre are most commonly mirrored. Copies of intonation markers can be recreated.

- **Value and belief mirroring:** In this case, the therapist should initially identify any key values and beliefs held by the patient and then directly or indirectly validate them through verbal and non-verbal communication. For example, if it is discovered that the patient is interested in art and painting, occasionally mentioning famous artists and their works can be effective.

Each type of rapport building has numerous intricacies in its application, and when used correctly, it can yield remarkable results in working with patients as well as in everyday interpersonal communication.

Eye Accessing Cues

The calibration technique in NLP is used to gather various verbal and non-verbal information for subsequent analysis and qualitative utilization in psychotherapeutic work. One of the most popular calibration models in NLP is the eye-accessing cues model, which has been extensively explored and developed by Robert Dilts. This model involves using information about the six main directions of the interlocutor's gaze, which often have specific, fixed meanings.

Eye movements play a significant role in our cognitive processes, particularly in the construction and recall of sensory experiences. They can provide valuable insights into how we visualize and remember visual images, construct sounds or speech, and connect with our bodily sensations. In this section, we will explore the different eye movements and their corresponding cognitive functions.

Let's examine these directions in more detail.

Upward and to the right gaze: When we shift our gaze upward and to the right, it is often associated with the construction of visual images. This cognitive process involves mentally creating or manipulating visual representations in our mind. It allows us to vividly imagine and construct new visual scenes or scenarios.	Upward and to the left gaze: On the other hand, when we direct our gaze upward and to the left, it is linked to the recall of visual images. This cognitive process involves retrieving previously stored visual memories, enabling us to remember and mentally recreate past visual experiences.
Rightward gaze: Turning our gaze solely to the right is related to the construction of sounds or speech. This cognitive function allows us to mentally generate or manipulate auditory stimuli, such as constructing inner dialogues or imagining different sounds.	**Leftward gaze:** Conversely, when we shift our gaze solely to the left, it is associated with the recall of sounds or speech. This cognitive process involves retrieving auditory memories, enabling us to remember and mentally replay past sounds or conversations.
Downward and to the right gaze: When we look downward and to the right, it involves connecting our visual experiences with bodily sensations. This cognitive function allows us to integrate or associate visual images with physical or sensory feelings, enhancing our overall sensory experience.	**Downward and to the left gaze:** Directing our gaze downward and to the left is linked to internal dialogue and reflection. This cognitive process involves engaging in introspection, self-reflection, or internal conversations with ourselves.

Table of Eye Accessing Cues Vectors

Understanding these various eye movements and their corresponding cognitive functions provides valuable insights into how our minds process and represent information. By studying these mechanisms, we can further comprehend the complex interplay between our sensory perceptions, memories, and internal cognitive processes.

According to Robert Dilts' assumptions, this pattern holds true for 70% of right-handed individuals. In the case of left-handed individuals, the right and left columns may be reversed. There are cases of specific individual variations, so this pattern should not be perceived as entirely universal. In the vast majority of cases, the following remains constant for this model: if a person's gaze is directed upward, it means they are processing visual images. If the gaze moves horizontally, the person is processing auditory or verbal representations. If the gaze is lowered, it indicates engagement with kinesthetic sensations or that the person is immersed in internal dialogue.

Representational Profiles of Personality

One of the key models of personality profiling in NLP is the representational systems model. There are four main representational profiles of personality: visual, auditory, kinesthetic, and digital. Belonging to a specific profile means that one's perception emphasizes a particular representational system. Pure profiles do not exist; we always utilize all sensations in our body. However, in some individuals, the emphasis is significantly shifted, allowing for the identification of distinct profiles. It is common to observe individuals who combine characteristics from different profiles.

Characteristics of individuals belonging to different representational profiles:

Visual

- Has a tendency to use visual language and expressions.
- Focuses on images, appearances, and visual aesthetics.
- Demonstrates a strong visual memory and vivid imagination.
- Pays attention to visual details and stimuli in their environment.

Auditory

- Uses auditory predicates and expressions in speech.
- Relies on sound, tone, and rhythm in communication.
- Has good auditory memory and a musical inclination.
- Notices and remembers auditory details and sounds in their surroundings.

Kinesthetic

- Prefers kinesthetic predicates and expressions.
- Values physical sensations, touch, and bodily experiences.
- Relates to emotions, feelings, and physical comfort.
- Demonstrates sensitivity to physical space and tactile stimuli.

Digital

- Utilizes cognitive and abstract predicates in speech.
- Emphasizes logical thinking, analysis, and categorization.
- Prefers intellectual discussions and problem-solving.
- Focuses on concepts, ideas, and mental processes.

Predicates of Speech

One of the earliest topics actively explored within the NLP tradition was speech predicates. The founders of NLP discovered that individuals who actively perceive and interact with the world through specific sensory modalities tend to use speech predicates corresponding to those modalities. The distribution of predicates across sensory modalities can be as follows:

Visual Predicates	Auditory Predicates	Kinesthetic Predicates	Digital Predicates
See, view, watch, observe, light, color, perspective, notice, examine, scrutinize, brightness, contrast, dimness, contemplate, review, gaze.	Listen, pay attention, sound, melodic, noisy, loud, ringing, buzzing, speaking, shouting, resonant, tone, intonation, timbre, noise.	Feel, sense, warm, soft, fluffy, smooth, springy, rigid, flexible, rough, touch, stroking, impact, push-off.	Calculate, transform, convert, ponder, reflect, contemplate, add, subtract, multiply, divide, compute, and create.

Table of Speech Predicates 1

In addition to the four main categories of predicates, within the realm of kinesthetics, we can distinguish completely separate and independent categories. These include motor, gustatory, olfactory, and vestibular predicates.

Motor Predicates	Gustatory Predicates	Gustatory Predicates	Vestibular Predicates
Move, shift, slide, walk, run, jump, approach, take off, fall, move.	Taste, taste, anticipate, deliciousness, sweet, bitter, salty, sour, overly sweet, spicy.	Smell, sniff, scent, fragrance, aroma, stench.	Balance, equilibrium, balance, rotate, spin, unwind, twist.

Table of Speech Predicates 2

The use of speech predicates related to motor actions allows us to describe and communicate experiences involving physical movement and actions. Gustatory predicates involve the perception of taste and flavor, enabling individuals to express their sensory experiences related to different tastes. Olfactory predicates are used to convey the sense of smell and the perception of different odors. Lastly, vestibular predicates pertain to balance, equilibrium, and the physical sensations associated with movements and rotation.

By understanding and utilizing these various speech predicates, therapists can better align their communication with the sensory modalities and subjective experiences of their clients, facilitating effective therapeutic interventions.

There is a greater number of predicates that correspond to each representational system than we present in the tables.

The more developed a person's particular representational system is, the more frequently they use predicates that align with it, and the greater the number of predicates within that representational system they employ. Predicates associated with the preferred representational system evoke positive, sometimes euphoric, states in individuals. Predicates from a less-utilized representational system may have no impact on the person at all. If a visually oriented individual prefers the phrase "I see bright prospects for our communication" in their communication, a kinesthetic individual is more likely to say, "I feel that we have a significant number of points of connection." By knowing a person's preferred representational system, we can automatically establish rapport with them by using predicates that correspond to their system. The study of various speech predicates is applicable in the context of trance induction. If a hypnotherapist utilizes a wide range of speech predicates during the trance induction process, it can create a unique volume and depth of the hypnotic trance.

Sensory Strategies

While examining how people utilize their sensations to perceive the world, the creators of NLP discovered that individuals tend to employ specific chains of sensations to achieve fixed outcomes. These chains of sensations are referred to as sensory strategies, and there are a multitude of such strategies among individuals. Some strategies yield successful, constructive outcomes, while others do not. Let's explore these sensory strategies:

1. **Decision Strategy:** This involves the sensations an individual experiences when making a specific decision. For example, a person may first need to visualize an image and then feel the sensations that arise in their body. If the sensations are positive, they proceed with the action; otherwise, they halt the action.

2. **Reality Strategy:** This strategy enables individuals to judge the reality or unreality of their perceptions. For instance, how can we differentiate between what is real and what is not? Memories of yesterday or a dream that occurred last night? The sensory strategies for this test can be highly diverse. For example, a person may recall

a series of past images that evoke a positive kinesthetic response, indicating those with the highest likelihood of being real. Then they recall an image that is subjected to the test of realism. Subsequently, a kinesthetic test is performed for this image to determine the difference in kinesthetic response compared to the images that are considered highly realistic. If there is a clear match, the image is categorized as real; otherwise, it is deemed unreal.

3. **Creativity Strategy:** This strategy pertains to how a creative individual generates something new. An example of this strategy can be seen in Salvador Dali's creative process. He would sit in front of a canvas, place a metal basin in front of him, and hold a spoon above the basin. He would then wait for drowsiness to set in, reaching a semi-dream state. When he fell asleep, the spoon would fall into the metal basin, creating a loud clang. Dali would wake up, derive images, and start painting based on the sensations and states that arose from this experience.

4. **Motivation Strategy:** This strategy explores how we can motivate ourselves to take action. A powerful motivational strategy was discovered by boxer Mike Tyson. Describing his experience, he said, "When I hit rock bottom and had no strength or desire to continue my training, I would look into my future and tell myself: if you don't get up and keep going, tomorrow will be even worse."

5. **Memory Strategy:** This is the ability to memorize blocks of information. John Grinder once proposed an interesting strategy for remembering the names of unfamiliar people.

According to his suggestion, during an introduction, upon hearing the person's name, you first visualize the name written on their forehead, then pronounce the name aloud several times, and finally make a hand gesture as if you are writing their name on paper.

6. **Thinking Strategy:** An example of a thinking strategy is the approach to solving life problems or gaining understanding. For instance, the creator of provocative therapy, Frank Farrelly, mentioned that during a therapeutic session, numerous internal monitors appear in his mind, each showing a variation of behavior that can be employed in working with the patient. When he makes a choice, he associates it with the corresponding image and proceeds to manifest what he has envisioned.

By incorporating these sensory strategies into our understanding, we can gain insights into how individuals perceive and interact with the world around them. Moreover, recognizing and utilizing these strategies can enhance communication and facilitate the achievement of desired outcomes.

We have provided only five examples of sensory strategies, but there are a multitude of existing strategies in total.

Sensory strategies can be modified, thereby bringing about significant behavioral changes in individuals. By transmitting one person's strategy to another, we can effectively teach them to perform certain tasks with greater proficiency and efficiency. The strategies we have described may involve both sensory structures, which are literal sequences of sensations, and fixed meanings associated with the context of their implementation. In its literal sense, a sensory strategy refers solely to a sequence of sensations. During the process of modeling sensory experience in NLP, sensory strategies are marked by a sequence of Latin letters, representing the utilized representational systems.

To effectively understand and analyze sensory experiences, it is essential to have a comprehensive system for encoding and representing sensory strategies. The following table presents the coding system for sensory strategies, along with their representative systems.

Notation	Representative System
Ve, Vi	Visual External, Visual Internal
At, Ad	Auditory Tonal, Auditory Discrete
K	Kinesthetic
M	Motor
G	Gustatory
O	Olfactory
Vs	Vestibular
N	Nociceptive (Pain)

Table of Encoding for Sensory Strategies

*The letter "**e**" represents external sensory experiences, while "**i**" denotes internal sensory experiences. The letter "**t**" signifies tonal* *or auditory aspects, while "**d**" represents discrete or digital elements.*

By utilizing this notation system, we can categorize and describe various sensory strategies. Here is an example of a sensory strategy notation and its potential interpretation:

Example: Ve → Vi → K → Adi → Ade

Interpretation: The individual visually perceives an external image → mentally represents possible future actions or interactions with the image → experiences a kinesthetic response to the perceived image → reflects on the sensations evoked → articulates a conclusion.

Sensory strategies can vary in complexity, ranging from simple combinations of a few elements to intricate algorithms with multiple branches and steps. Understanding and deciphering these strategies is crucial for comprehending how individuals process and respond to sensory information.

Neurological Levels

One of the most widely used models in NLP at present is the model of neurological levels (NL), which provides some insights into the logical levels of personality and their semantic content. The term "neuro" suggests that the very process of structuring personality and various cognitive and behavioral processes associated with this structuring have a direct relationship to physiological processes, particularly neurological processes. This model is effectively employed both in the process of modeling the experiences of different individuals and in the development of various therapeutic techniques aimed at constructive personality change.

Neurological levels provide a framework for understanding the different levels of human experience and identity. Each level corresponds to specific aspects of a person's being and can offer insights into their deeper motivations, values, and beliefs. The following table outlines the key characteristics associated with each neurological level. The NL model encompasses six core levels.

Level	Key Characteristics
6. Mission and Vision	This level addresses the larger abstract roles that can be inherent to a person's identity. It delves into existential, transpersonal, and philosophical aspects of the self. Question: "**Who am I in a broader sense beyond the social roles I play?**"
5. Identity	This level pertains to the specific identities and roles that shape an individual's sense of self. Question: "**Who am I?**"
4. Values and Beliefs	This level explores the values and beliefs that underlie one's manifested behaviors. Question: "**What is important and valuable?**"
3. Capabilities	This level focuses on specific qualities of behavior and performance. Question: "**How does something happen?**"
2. Actions	This level involves the immediate actions or behaviors being exhibited. Question: "**What is happening?**"
1.Environment	This level considers the context and circumstances in which events occur. Question: "**Where and when does something happen?**"

Neurological Levels Table

Understanding these neurological levels provides valuable insights into the various dimensions of human experience. By examining these levels, we can gain a comprehensive understanding of an individual's identity, motivations, and the underlying factors that shape their behavior.

One practical application of NLP is the classification of patient therapy requests. Each request can be attributed to a specific neurological level, and based on that level, specific therapeutic techniques can be selected that are most appropriate for addressing the request. For example:

1. **Environment-level request**: "I'm fed up with the people around me."
2. **Action-level request**: "I want to get rid of anxiety."
3. **Capabilities-level request**: "My spouse doesn't treat me well."
4. **Values and beliefs-level request**: "I don't understand why women don't like me."
5. **Identity-level request**: "I want to fully mature as a person."
6. **Mission and vision-level request**: "I want to contribute something special to the world."

By classifying therapy requests according to their corresponding neurological levels, therapists can tailor their approach to address the specific needs of each patient. This targeted application of NLP techniques enhances the effectiveness of therapy interventions.

One example of therapeutic application using NL is the practice of "aligning neurological levels." It is believed that all NLs are closely interconnected, with higher levels influencing the lower ones. Thus, if a patient's request is received at a lower NL, the therapist can help the patient move to a higher level of personality. This process involves exploring the necessary states and insights that can be brought to the lower logical levels. It can serve as a resourceful element for transforming both symptoms and the individual as a whole.

Neurological alignment can be conducted through regular conversation, but the classic approach involves using anchoring techniques for anchoring and the subsequent introduction of states.

For example, if a patient's request is at the Behavior Level and stated as "I want to get rid of anxiety," the therapist can systematically elevate the patient to higher levels.

Transitioning to the Capabilities and Skills Level activates the specific details of how anxiety arises within the individual and its nature.

Transitioning to the Beliefs and Values Level brings awareness of their content in the context of personal anxiety.

Transitioning to the Identity Level allows full recognition of the social roles in which anxiety manifests.

Transitioning to the sixth level provides awareness of the larger purpose behind fulfilling these social roles. Sometimes it is necessary to reach the sixth level, while in other cases, activating the fifth level may be sufficient. When the fifth or sixth level is reached, its state is anchored, often through a kinesthetic anchor.

Naturally, before anchoring, it is necessary to ensure that the achieved state is resourceful and serves as a "meta" state in relation to the stated condition. With the anchored meta-state of a higher NL, the descent is carried out sequentially to a lower one. If the sixth level has been reached, the descent is made to the fifth; if the fifth level has been reached, the descent is made to the fourth, and so on. During the descent to a lower NL, the anchor of the meta-state that was reached earlier is activated.

Thus, the therapist and the patient descend to the symptom-level NL and introduce the meta-state there as well. If necessary, it is possible to go to lower levels than the one from which the request was expressed and introduce the meta-state there. This is an approximate description of how neurological alignment can occur. This practice may have nuances and specific features that need to be taken into account when working with patients of different psychological profiles.

Milton Model

The two main founders of NLP, Richard Bandler and John Grinder, were introduced to one of the most renowned American hypnotherapists, Milton Erickson, through their friend and mentor, Gregory Bateson.

According to legend, they studied with him and modeled his skills for approximately 11 months, after which they started incorporating numerous patterns of his work with patients into NLP.

The modeled therapy patterns of Milton Erickson were subsequently named the Milton Model and included patterns specifically related to hypnotic interactions with patients.

It is worth noting that Erickson did not limit himself to the use of hypnosis alone; thus, his range of therapeutic methods was significantly broader than what is considered within the scope of the Milton Model.

The Milton Model is mainly adapted for application within the context of hypnotic suggestion.

Let's identify the main patterns of the Milton Model:

1. **Rapport with existing experience:** During trance induction, vague clarifying questions are asked, allowing the interlocutor some freedom of choice.

Questions like "Isn't it?" or "Isn't it so?"

2. **Double binds:** The interlocutor is offered two or more choices without actually choosing. In other words, no matter what the interlocutor chooses, the choice will always lead to the correct outcome.
   Example: "Will you enter a hypnotic trance right now or when you sit comfortably and relax?"

3. **Conversational presuppositions:** This pattern actively uses modal operators of possibility, giving a sense of freedom of choice and the absence of rigid constraints.
   Example: "Can you allow yourself to enter a trance state? Can your unconscious start learning? Is healing possible in this hypnotic trance?"

4. **Extended quotes:** This pattern extends the frame of quoting and prolongs it until the interlocutor's attention is slightly overloaded. Typically, during extended quotes, the contexts of description are sequentially changed, creating additional load on the perceptual apparatus. Due to the overload, what was said earlier gradually fades into the unconscious. This, in fact, is the goal of using this pattern.
   Example: "I recently remembered a patient who told me a story from his childhood. He met a boy who once climbed a mountain and saw an amazing view that immersed him in a very pleasant and relaxed state, akin to a deep and vivid dream that some people can experience..."

5. **Selective violation of boundaries:** In this pattern, we begin to attribute cognitive processes, emotions, states,

and sensations to objects that cannot experience them. Thus, two goals are achieved. Firstly, the perception pattern is disrupted, indirectly suggesting what we would like our interlocutor to experience.
Example: "I wonder what the chair can feel like when someone enters a hypnotic trance on it?"

6. **Uncertainty pauses:** During the construction of a sentence, we pause for a while, allowing the interlocutor's imagination to fill it in independently in their mind, and then we complete it.
Example: "As you enter a hypnotic trance, you may feel... a special gift from your unconscious."

7. **Utilization:** Whatever happens to the interlocutor during communication, whatever resistance they may exert, it can be utilized. That is, we can gain control without directly confronting the problematic behavior.
Example, if a patient tells the therapist, "I can't enter a hypnotic trance," the therapist responds, "That's right, you can't enter a hypnotic trance until you sit in that chair."

8. **Analog marking:** Analog marking can be of three main types: visual, auditory, and kinesthetic. During visual marking, when suggesting certain words, for example, we make a specific gesture visible to the interlocutor. During auditory marking, we change the tone, volume, or intonation of speech. During kinesthetic marking, we may specifically touch the interlocutor. Auditory analog marking is most commonly used during trance induction.

9. **Linguistic linkage:** To create a coherent flow of trance induction, linking words like "and," "but," as well as phrases indicating cause-and-effect relationships, such as "when-then," "if-then," "while," and "during," are used.
   Examples: "As you enter the trance and feel relaxation, you can let go of your thoughts. You may resist and keep your eyes open, but your unconscious has already started to immerse you in a hypnotic trance. When you feel my touch on your shoulder, you will begin to experience something new and unusual."

10. **Temporal ambiguity:** The use of words that establish an indefinite temporal framework.
    Examples: "Sometimes it happens... Occasionally, the unconscious reveals its secrets... There are moments when the trance simply emerges..."

11. **Addressing personality parts:** Direct or indirect addressing of a specific part of the personality. This breaks the interlocutor's perception pattern and significantly enhances the trance effect of communication.
    Example: "I greet your unconscious. Your wise part is ready to manifest. What would your symptom like to tell you?"

12. **Hypnotic approval:** Words of approval for the experience that an individual goes through during hypnotic induction.
    Examples: "Very good... Exactly... That's right..."

NLP, as an integrative psychotherapy, naturally goes beyond

existing models and constantly evolves, introducing new models of change and transformation. In NLP, we primarily see not just a psychotherapy system, but rather an operating system that enables more effective interaction with both our conscious and unconscious realms.

It is worth emphasizing once again that NLP is not simply a collection of techniques and models but rather a specific metaphilosophy that allows for more effective interaction with new experiences, qualitatively assimilating them into our consciousness, and transmitting them to others in various life contexts.

Metaprograms

In the early 1980s, when NLP had already been actively developing for many years, it was discovered that different NLP techniques produced rapid and profound changes for some individuals while being less effective for others. This led to the idea that there were certain omissions at the foundation of NLP models. There must be filters that could reliably determine which types of techniques are more or less effective in different cases. Simply dividing people into visual, auditory, kinesthetic, and digital (VAKD) profiles was not sufficient, although these profile filters had significant value. To some extent, the idea of meta-programs was likely borrowed from Osgood's semantic differentials and cognitive styles initially mentioned by Alfred Adler. Although the ideas of cognitive styles were later extensively developed by a range of authors.

Regardless, it is important to highlight the relationship between the concepts of meta-programs, semantic differentials, and cognitive styles since a deeper examination of research dedicated to these concepts can provide a wealth of useful and complementary information. In the next part of this chapter, where we will explore Ken Wilber's integrative model in more detail, we will provide a more comprehensive description of cognitive styles. In the context of the chapter dedicated to

NLP, we would like to examine 15 fundamental meta-programs that, in my opinion, are most applicable in practical work. It is worth noting that one of the NLP researchers and trainers, Michael Hall, in his book "The Secrets of Personal Mastery: 51 Metaprograms," describes the corresponding number of meta-programs in its title and provides a detailed analysis.

First and foremost, it is important to note that meta-programs are filters in our perceptual apparatus that allow us to better perceive certain blocks of information while disregarding others. Depending on our understanding of how these filters function, we can more effectively deliver information to individuals and interact with them. In the context of NLP practice, it has been discovered that meta-programs can not only be verified through interaction with individuals but also changed. This has led to the development of new techniques and practices.

List of Metaprograms

1. **Sorting Filters** (people, values, processes/procedures, actions/things):
   What is the primary focus of attention for a person? For example, if you are going on vacation, are you primarily going to be with someone? Or with whom? Or is it important in the context of your life? For example, a pilgrimage to holy places. Or are you going to do something? For example, simply surfing. Or are you going with the intention of improving a skill? Or towards a particular thing or for a specific item? These are all sorting filters. People have them in different combinations. If the sorting filters of two people do not match at all, the

likelihood of their meeting can be highly doubtful.

2. **Chunk Size** (big, small):
Some people are accustomed to thinking in large categories of experience and abstract terms, generalizing blocks of their experience into them. Others, on the contrary, love to detail their experience. A vivid example can be a phrase from one person to another: "Buy something tasty." This phrase clearly corresponds to a large chunk size. And a person with a specific metaprogram profile criterion will use it. If a person with a small chunk size hears this phrase, it can greatly confuse them.

3. **Thinking Style** (deductive, inductive, or transductive):
Some people have a well-developed deductive thinking style, thinking from the general to the specific. For example, if you know that a person suffers from schizophrenia and understand the criteria for its manifestation, you can easily predict how the patient will behave in different situations. Others have a well-developed inductive thinking style, thinking from specific to general. For example, if you are trying to verify if someone is lying in their communication and gather several clear signs of deception, you can label the person as a liar based on the generalization of these signs. And for some individuals, transductive thinking can be well-developed, thinking in terms of analogies and metaphors. For example, if you are a psychotherapist and a patient with depression comes to you, you can quickly recall all the cases when patients with depression came to you or remember cases of depression described in various

psychotherapeutic literature. In the case of transduction, you remain at the same logical level of generalization and operate with the information contained within it.

4. **Comparison Focus** (similarity-difference):
   Some people, in the process of communicating with others, more often activate the confirmation filter that looks for similarities between themselves and their interlocutor. Others do the opposite; they constantly seek differences.

5. **Motivation Type** (towards positive or away from negative, towards positive and then away from negative, away from negative and then towards positive):
   For some people, to start moving towards a goal, they need to anticipate the joy of achieving it. For others, they need to feel how unpleasant it would be if they stayed put. For others, they need to first anticipate the benefits and then feel the discomfort if there is no progress. And there are those who are the opposite; for motivation, they first need to experience the potential negative outcome if there is no movement and only then understand that moving towards the goal can yield very good results.

6. **Type of Reference** (internal, external - others, external - world):
   When we experience positive or negative outcomes in our lives, we tend to attribute various causes to these results. Individuals with an internal reference type believe that they are solely responsible for everything, while those with an external reference type, oriented towards other people, shift the responsibility onto others. Individuals with an

external reference type towards the world believe that everything happening in the world is related to destiny, circumstances, the intervention of mystical forces, and so on.

7. **Orientation in Time** (past, present, and future):
   In our lives, we can be more or less focused on different temporal periods. Some people derive pleasure from being surrounded by old things and watching old movies, embracing the nostalgia of the past. Others are oriented towards the present moment, interested in what has just been released, the latest trends, or recent updates to stay in sync with the times. Yet, there are those who strive to surround themselves with objects and images that anticipate what the world of the future might be like.

8. **Temporal Inclusion** (inclusion of time, temporal dissociation):
   Individuals with temporal inclusion experience a life where fragments of memories are closely associated. They derive more sensations from life but are less inclined to reflect on exactly what is happening or contextually analyze the situation. Conversely, individuals with temporal dissociation are always somewhat detached from their feelings, better analyzing the current life context, their memories, and their potential future.

9. **Temporal Accessibility** (sequential, random):
   Individuals with sequential temporal accessibility constantly strive to bring order to the sequence of their life experiences; they have a preference for order. On the other

hand, individuals with random temporal accessibility are not burdened with the need to clearly and structuredly organize their life experiences.

10. **Information Gathering Style** (uptime, downtime): People with an up-to-date information-gathering style are predominantly oriented towards the external world. They are highly vigilant, capable of noticing even the slightest differences and changes in the world in general, and in people's behavior in particular. Conversely, individuals with a downtime information-gathering style have their attention focused inward. They find it more difficult to gather new information but possess remarkable abilities to analyze the information they already have, draw accurate logical conclusions, and make inferences.

11. **Perceptual Categories** (polarity, continuum): Some individuals tend to perceive the world as a set of rigid polarities. For them, things are either good or bad, completely acceptable or completely unacceptable, excellent or terrible. This perceptual category is characterized by polarity. On the other hand, others are capable of thinking more smoothly and moderately. Such individuals judge something as more or less suitable, to a large extent uncomfortable, acceptable to 80%, and so on. They have more differentiated scales of evaluation.

12. **Perceptual Resilience** (penetrability, impermeability): Individuals with the metaprogram of "perceptual resilience and penetrability" experience strong discomfort when even the slightest distractions arise during the

process of engaging with or focusing on something. They can be irritated by a slight rustle behind the door, a sudden noise outside, a barely audible conversation in another room, and so on.
On the other hand, individuals with the metaprogram of "perceptual resilience—impermeability" perceive things differently. They can calmly concentrate on solving a task even in an environment with numerous distracting factors. During the task, these factors simply cease to bother them.

13. **Modal Operators** (necessity, possibility):
When we consider the modal operator of necessity as a metaprogram, we refer to situations where a person follows the impulse of obligation, a sense of self-compulsion in certain life situations. For such individuals, a life situation is more of a duty than a freedom of choice, and the dominant phrase is "I must." Conversely, individuals with the metaprogram "modal operator - possibility" perceive the world as an arena of possibilities and freedom of choice rather than duty and adherence to it. Their key phrase is "I can."

14. **Comparison Style** (quantitative, qualitative):
For some individuals, the most significant criterion for task completion is quantitative indicators. For example, they may focus on having dealt with 20 patients, running 50 kilometers, eating 5 apples, and so on. When the metaprogram "comparison style - quantitative" dominates, the quality of the performance itself may not be particularly in focus. On the other hand, individuals with the metaprogram "comparison style - qualitative"

prioritize immediate quality in the execution of tasks. For them, it's not about how many times they perform a certain physical exercise but how well and qualitatively they do it.

15. **Orientation Towards Closure** (completeness, incompleteness):
    Some individuals are deeply concerned about ensuring that everything they start is completed. Unfinished tasks weigh heavily on them, making them restless. This metaprogram is known as "orientation towards closure - completeness." In contrast, individuals with the opposing metaprogram do not experience discomfort when they initiate a task and leave it unfinished.

In NLP, there are no notions of good or bad metaprograms. There are no boundaries defining correctness or incorrectness. In the context of modeling mastery or pathology, one can create a metaprogram profile of an individual and empirically observe how specific sets of metaprograms can lead to various outcomes.

Integral Philosophy of Ken Wilber

Only a portion of Ken Wilber's life was dedicated to psychotherapy. He is not the creator of any specific school of psychotherapy; however, his integrative philosophical approach has already made a significant contribution to psychotherapeutic practice, in my opinion. Ken Wilber's theoretical models are remarkably capable of organizing the vast conglomerate of experience accumulated by various schools of psychotherapy into comprehensive models and structures. In his philosophy, Ken Wilber is closely aligned with NLP as a form of specific meta-philosophy, although he does not have a direct association with it.

Kenneth Earl Wilber II was born in 1949 in Oklahoma City, USA. Due to his father's military service in the US Air Force, Wilber's family constantly moved when he was a child. Wilber completed high school in Lincoln, Nebraska. He demonstrated himself as an extraordinary and highly gifted child in school, grasping various subjects effortlessly and even earning the nickname "Brain." Wilber excelled in sports disciplines such as football, volleyball, and basketball. He also showed talent as a gymnast and track athlete.

Ken Wilber

In 1967, at the insistence of his parents, Wilber enrolled in Duke University's medical school to study medicine. However, he quickly became disillusioned with the chosen profession and transferred to the University of Nebraska, where he soon obtained a bachelor's degree in chemistry and biology. Alongside his studies in chemistry and biology, Wilber devoted considerable attention to psychology and Eastern philosophy. After completing his academic education, he made the decision to fully focus on his writing career.

In 1972, Wilber met his future wife, Emmy Watts, whom he married the same year.

At the age of 23, in 1973, he completed his first book, "The Spectrum of Consciousness," which became his initial attempt to create and describe an integrative model that unifies Western and Eastern philosophical perspectives. However, for a long time, many publishing houses refused to publish this book due to its perceived complexity. It was only in 1977 that it was published by the Theosophical Publishing House, "Quest Books." The publication of this book brought recognition to the author in academic circles, enabling him to start delivering various lectures and seminars on the material described in the book.

In 1978, Wilber organized the release of the transpersonal journal "ReVision."

In 1979, his second book, "No Boundary," was published. This was followed by the publication of "The Atman Project" in 1980 and "Up from Eden" in 1981.

In 1981, Wilber divorced his wife, Emmy, and moved to Cambridge, Massachusetts, where he continued publishing the journal "ReVision."

In 1983, Wilber met his second wife, Terry Killam. After marrying Terry, she was diagnosed with breast cancer, which led Wilber to entirely put aside his writing career from 1984 to 1987 in order to dedicate himself to caring for his ill wife. However, Terry's treatment did not yield significant results, and she passed away in 1989. Based on the experience gained during Terry's treatment and care, Wilber published the book "Grace and Grit" in 1991.

In 1998, Ken Wilber founded the Integral Institute, which focused on various research endeavors and the development of scientific inquiries aimed at integration into a theoretical model that allows for the synthesis of scientific knowledge into comprehensive and structured models.

In 1999, Wilber published another book titled "Integral Psychology," in which he attempted to present models that encompassed the diverse psychological knowledge available at that time.

In 2000, Wilber released his next book, "A Theory of Everything," where he conducted an integrative analysis of various spheres of human activity, such as politics, religion, science, and business. He demonstrated how these spheres could be represented through the lens of Clare Graves' spiral dynamics.

In 2006, Wilber published his book "Integral Spirituality," which became a remarkable synthesis of his ideas on spirituality and religion in diverse mystical traditions from around the world. It is worth noting that Wilber not only explored these traditions on a theoretical level but also immersed himself deeply in many of them, gaining practical experience. Thus, we are dealing with not just a theoretical compilation but also a living experience, making the material, in my opinion, even more unique.

Since 1987 and up to the present day, Ken Wilber has been living and working in Denver, Colorado, where he leads the activities of the Integral Institute and University, both of which are actively developing, and whose research findings are increasingly being applied in various spheres of human life.

Ken Wilber's integral approach finds its embodiment in a wide range of scientific investigations, extending far beyond mere philosophy. Wilber introduced the philosophy of integration into areas such as psychology, psychotherapy, philosophy, sociology, politics, economics, religion, mysticism, and more.

Studying various schools of psychology and psychotherapy with their diverse theoretical concepts and practical techniques, Ken Wilber observed that each of them has its own validity. They do not contradict one another but rather complement each other qualitatively. Wilber proposed a spectral model to examine these theories, suggesting that schools of psychology and psychotherapy are like colors in a rainbow, existing within their own spectra. According to him, only by considering the entirety of the spectrum can one obtain a truly comprehensive picture of reality. Due to his deep fascination with various religious and mystical traditions, many researchers have attributed to Wilber the role of a transpersonal philosopher. However, Wilber's orientation was not merely towards the integration of Western and Eastern knowledge. His ideas aimed at integrating experiences from diverse fields of study and religions. Therefore, it would be incorrect to label Wilber as a transpersonal psychologist or philosopher. Wilber is a pure integrative philosopher.

One of the key models created by Ken Wilber is the AQAL model, which essentially became the foundation for his future theoretical and practical constructions. As his knowledge expanded, he further developed this model into AQALALASAT, which stands for "All Quadrants, All Levels, All Lines, All States, All Types."

The model itself, as conceived by Wilber, includes five distinct categories of experience that cannot be simplified and must be considered when examining experiences from an integrative standpoint.

Basic quadrants, also referred to as sectors, are four in total. The first sector is the "**I** - Individual Interior," focusing on the subjective experience of the individual. This sector encompasses realms such as religion, philosophy, subjective psychology, and phenomenology—essentially all areas of activity that primarily deal with subjective, rather than empirical, experience. The second sector is the "**It** - Individual Exterior," encompassing areas of activity that, on the one hand, study the individual but, on the other hand, have a direct relation to empirical, objectively verifiable experience.

This sector includes physiology, medicine, physics, chemistry, objective psychology, and so on. The third sector, the

"**We** - Collective Interior," pertains to the study of internal processes of group interaction among individuals. This sector encompasses fields such as cultural studies, sociology, cultural anthropology, and the like. The fourth sector, "**Its** - Collective Exterior," examines forms of activity that study external group social processes. This sector includes economics, politics, theories of system functioning, and the like.

Developmental levels imply a specific sequence of development that an individual or a group of individuals undergo during phylogenesis and ontogenesis. Developmental levels can be diverse. The scales of levels most commonly used by Wilber include the scales of value-motivational hierarchy by Clare Graves, the spiral dynamics by Don Beck and Chris Cowan, and the developmental levels proposed by Jane Loevinger, Robert Kegan, and Jean Gebser.

Developmental lines denote various forms of the ability to apply the intellectual sphere of personality. Each person and group of people, as they progress in their development, advance in their understanding of something to a certain extent. Some individuals excel in interpersonal communication, others solve mathematical equations, and others possess exceptional self-regulation abilities, and so on. Let us enumerate the main developmental lines:

1. **Cognitive** line, or the awareness of what exists.
   Cognitive and mathematical intelligence.
2. **Moral** line, or the awareness of how things should be.
   Moral intelligence.
3. **Emotional** line. Awareness and influence on the spectrum of emotions, self-regulation.
   Emotional intelligence.

4. **Interpersonal** line, the ability to communicate effectively with others.
   Social intelligence.
5. **Needs** line, exemplified by Maslow's hierarchy of needs model:
   recognition of personal needs and the strategies to fulfill them.
   Needs intelligence.
6. **Spiritual** line. Awareness of the purpose of one's existence.
   Spiritual intelligence.

And numerous other potential developmental lines.

States can occur in all quadrants and can be categorized as states of consciousness—wakefulness, dreaming, and trance (the "**I** - Individual Interior" sector)—and states of energy—gross, subtle, and causal (the **"It** - Individual Exterior" sector). In the context of state analysis, Ken Wilber presents his classification of categories of spiritual states. It is also worth noting that states of consciousness can be peak, altered, religious, or meditative. All these states can be interpreted as spiritual.

Types also exist in all quadrants. A prominent example of a type is the masculine and feminine personality types. It can manifest in individuals or specific groups of people. For example, the masculine type of personality may involve identification with action, rigidity, and aggressiveness, while the feminine type is associated with communication, overall sociability, empathy, and compassion. Here, we can recall Carl Jung's typology of individuals as extroverts and introverts, which he later expanded by adding four more profiles—people of thinking, intuition, sensing, and feeling—and each of these can be viewed through the lens of introversion and extroversion. Based on Jung's typology, the Myers-Briggs Type Indicator and Aushra Augustinavichute's socionics were created. Cognitive styles, which may be inherent to a person, can also be considered as part of personality typology. For example, the Enneagram model and Enneatypes developed by Oscar Ichazo.

Let us now examine in more detail some of the models that Ken Wilber actively considers within his AQAL framework.

Application of Quadrants

The application of quadrants can be utilized in various spheres of human activity, including psychology, psychotherapy, medicine, business, and politics. Quadrants provide a remarkable dimension of attention that can be taken into account when addressing a wide range of tasks.

"**I** - Individual Interior" Quadrant: Psychoanalysis, Gestalt therapy, Humanistic therapy, Provocative therapy.	"**It** - Individual Exterior" Quadrant: Behavioral therapy, Pharmaceutical assistance, Biological feedback.
"**We** - Collective Interior" Quadrant: Psychodrama, Family psychotherapy, Systemic constellations, Group analysis, Alcoholics Anonymous groups.	"**Its** - Collective Exterior" Quadrant: Social support and assistance services, Anonymous helpline services, Programs for predicting various mental disorders and problems with social adaptation.

Four Quadrants of Integral Psychotherapy

(Here, we can observe how various therapeutic practices and

schools of therapy are distributed among the quadrants.)

When examining reality through the lens of only one sector, we may fall into various forms of radicalism that can limit our perception of the reality map. Let's consider the examples of the four main radicalisms.

"**I** - Individual Interior" Quadrant: Radical idealism. "Reality is mind".	"**It** - Individual Exterior" Quadrant: Behavioral therapy, Pharmaceutical assistance, Biological feedback.
"**We** - Collective Interior" Quadrant: Radical postmodernism, "Reality is meanings constructed by culture".	"**Its** - Collective Exterior" Quadrant: Radical systems theory, "Reality is the web of life".

Levels of Development by Jean Gebser

Jean Gebser identified five main levels of development that, on the one hand, are reflected in the process of phylogenesis, and on the other hand, can be traced in the context of social development from early childhood to adulthood. He distinguished five stages: archaic, magic, mythical, rational, and integrative stages. They primarily reflect the dynamics of human development based on the dynamics of epochs, millennia, and centuries.

Archaic Stage: The state at this stage is fully identical to the world - a complete merging and undividedness with the world. At the level of personal development, it is the complete symbiosis of the infant with the mother. At this stage, there is no real need to influence anything. Symbiotic connection with the environment is a specific guarantee for solving key life tasks. It is a state of absolute infantilism and innocence. The first early tribes that existed 500,000 years ago.

Magic Stage: At this stage, we already see not a literal identity with the world but unity with it. The first signs of differentiation and separation appear. At this stage, our ancestors existed with a special state of consciousness that had deep connections with nature. Jean Gebser introduces a special term for this stage - "vegetative interpenetration," indicating a subtle sense of interconnectedness among all living things. Vegetative interpenetration constitutes the essence of experiencing the world at this stage of development. In many ways, Gebser equates the state of vegetative interpenetration with Carl Jung's term "synchronicity," which refers to the profound mystical interconnectedness of everything in the world that cannot be grasped through rational constructs and concepts. At this stage, there emerges a mystical confidence in the ability to influence the world, although actions are still infantile. This is the stage of primary magical rituals and the beginning of sympathetic magic, where there may be a conviction that if an image of a deer is drawn before hunting and then struck with a spear, it will make the hunt more successful. Approximate time frame: 50,000–10,000 BCE.

Mythical Stage: At this stage, there is an even greater detachment from the world. Notions of various forms of duality in consciousness emerge, such as good and evil, light and dark, masculine and feminine. Full-fledged mythological descriptions of the world with pantheons of deities arise, whom one can serve and ask for something by performing specific rituals and adhering to rules, making one's life better and more correct. The first signs of the emergence of rational thinking may be observed, but they do not yet dominate or determine the main course of social events. Myth governs human consciousness. When problems arise, people turn to the divine and powerful entities in their beliefs, seeking a personalized factor that can solve their problems. Approximate time frame: 10,000-1,225 BCE.

Rational Stage: This stage is characterized by consciousness and the ego as something separate, differentiated, and autonomous. There is a need for clear temporal ordering in a linear formation. There is a clear demarcation of the past, present, and future. In previous stages, the state of "here-and-now" predominated, and the division into temporal periods was highly conditional. Human attention increasingly focuses on the details of acquired experience and its analysis, giving rise to scientific and exploratory forms of activity. According to Gebser, the approximate beginning of this stage is 1,225 BCE. In 1,336 BCE, according to Gebser, the rational stage enters a certain deficit period. At this stage, consciousness achieves final "liberation" from its origins.

Integral Stage: At this stage, we can observe the manifestation of going beyond the traditional perspective. The source begins to be perceived as something spiritual and tangible, capable of providing a sense of wholeness. Integrative notions of the world and human beings emerge. Various sciences and spiritual traditions gradually move towards integration and the unification of experience.

Levels of Ego Development by Jane Levinger

The origins of Jane Levinger's ideas about levels of ego development can be traced back to Alfred Adler. Adler was the first to express his ideas about the ego's ability to play a dominant role in relation to the realm of motivation. In her model, Levinger describes individual levels of personality maturity and the general tendency toward self-regulation. Levinger directly associates the process of ego development with the gradual acquisition of autonomy skills, which begin to manifest in behavior and constructively shape the surrounding world. In her classification, Levinger avoids rigid attachment to a fixed chronological age. Her model reflects a clear hierarchy of criteria that depicts the dynamics of personal maturation and one's capacity for autonomy. Each stage involves an examination of impulse control, the ability for adequate interpersonal relationships, self-awareness, and an analysis of one's behavior.

Levels of Development According to Levinger

1. **Pre-social stage**: At this stage, the infant gradually distinguishes itself from the surrounding world. There is a slow process of differentiation and self-awareness as a separate entity. Reality is constructed in the mind as a stable world of objects.

2. **Symbiotic stage**: The process of individuation continues. Although a close connection with the mother persists, there emerges a certain communicative sphere through the use of sound analog communication. The key to

transitioning to the next stage is the child's ability to express a literal or symbolic "no."

3. **Impulsive stage**: Various physical and emotional impulses that arise in the child's interaction with the external world contribute to their self-assertion as a separate entity. The focus is primarily on aggressive, alimentary, and sexual impulses. According to Levinger, the emergence of the word "why" in the child's lexicon serves as a trigger for transitioning to the next stage.

4. **Stage of self-defense**: The child begins to recognize the existing scheme of potential rewards and punishments and anticipates them. This leads to relative control over their behavior. Such control increasingly helps the child restrain the impulses that previously dominated their behavior in the earlier stage of development. At this stage, self-criticism is still absent, but the concepts of guilt and shame emerge. However, more often than not, the causes of guilt and shame are attributed to someone else or circumstances.

5. **Conformism stage**: This stage begins to actualize when the child establishes a connection between their own well-being and the well-being of the social group to which they belong. The rules of existence within the group become the leading value orientations, and their violation elicits serious disapproval. Group membership becomes a guarantee of personal safety and further development.

6. **Self-awareness stage**: At this stage, a vivid realization

emerges that the ideal self-image may not correspond to the image of the real self. Group stereotypes are gradually replaced by one's own stereotypes. Individual differences in character traits become apparent.

7. **Conscientiousness stage**: According to Levinger, this stage involves a radical complexity of the mechanisms of self-regulation. She also comments that very few individuals reach this stage by the age of 13-14. The stage of conscientiousness often marks the completion of a full internalization of social rules, where conscience, self-criticism, and a sense of responsibility begin to function fully. There is a need to set personal goals and strive to achieve them to the best of one's abilities and opportunities.

8. **Individualistic stage**: This stage particularly highlights the sense of personal individuality and poses challenges regarding emotional connections between people, issues of personal relationships, and ways to resolve them.

9. **Autonomous stage**: At this stage, the ability to embrace internal conflict emerges. It develops within the individual between their needs and the social obligations they undertake. A realistic view of the world, objectivity, and the ability to strive for abstract ideals and goals are formed.

10. **Integrated stage**: The key distinction of the integrated stage from the autonomous stage is the consolidation of a sense of identity. Levinger compares the integrated stage of development to Abraham Maslow's state of self-

actualization. According to Levinger, this stage of development is quite rare.

Stages of Human Development According to Robert Kegan

Robert Kegan, a professor at Harvard University, developed the theory of subject-object differentiation and orders of consciousness. Kegan identified a model of human developmental stages, incorporating five main stages into this model.

1. **Impulsive mind:** Early childhood. This stage is observed from birth to 5-6 years of age. The child's existence is determined by their momentary impulsive desires, which dominate over self-control.

2. **Imperial mind:** Adolescence (6% of the adult population). The approximate age range is from 6 to 20 years. The individual gradually gains control over their impulses and emotions, but their needs, interests, and desires captivate them. The ability to set specific goals and gradually achieve them emerges, as well as the need to adhere to social rules to avoid group censure.

3. **Socialized mind:** (58% of the adult population). This stage begins at the age of 20. The person gradually gains control over satisfying various social needs. They also become fully socialized and organize their life as part of society. At this stage, the influence of society on the individual, with its pros and cons, becomes fully revealed. This stage can continue throughout life.

4. **Self-authoring mind:** (35% of the adult population). At this stage, the individual gradually develops the ability to self-form, determine their environment, and follow their own path. They move away from conformist social rigidity characteristic of the previous stage.

5. **Self-transforming mind:** (1% of the adult population). At this level, fixation on oneself ceases. The individual is no longer consumed by ideas of satisfying their own needs. They perceive everything that manifests in the world and their life as equal and interdependent parts of a whole. This is a period of integrative and holistic perception of existence. These qualities are often found in various spiritual masters, philosophers, and highly intellectual individuals.

Spiral Dynamics by Don Beck and Chris Cowan

(Category of Developmental Levels)

Levels of Spiral Dynamics

1. **Beige**: The main idea of this level is to do whatever it takes to stay alive. It represents the level of physical survival. Instincts are used for survival purposes, and self-identity is very weak. The primary priorities are food, sex, warmth, and safety. It marks the transition from animal to human. Approximately 100,000 years ago.

2. **Purple**: Worshiping the spirits of nature and creating a

family hearth. Demonstrating subordination and loyalty to the leader and the group. Preserving sacred oaths. Strict obedience to accepted taboos and seasonal rituals. Basic self-identification emerges as part of the group. The main priorities are family, group affiliation, and adherence to rituals. The formation of tribes, magic, and primitive art. Approximately 50,000 years ago.

3. **Red**: The fundamental rule at this level is to be who you are and do whatever you want, regardless of anything else. Being in a constant state of readiness for battle. Striving for power and dominance over the group and other individuals. Seeking to impose one's own rules on the group in which one exists. The main priorities become power and dominance. The era of warlords, conquests, and discoveries. Approximately 10,000 years ago.

4. **Blue**: At this level, there is a desire to adhere to group rules and make sacrifices for them. Clear legal order. Subordination is directed more towards the group's rules than to the leader. Formation of clear moral principles. Establishment of bureaucracies. The emergence of a fully developed social matrix with clearly defined roles. Ideas of justice, democracy, and equality gain prominence. Living by the rules now provides the best opportunities for the future. Control of aggressive feelings. Emergence of literature, monotheism, and goal-oriented awareness. Approximately 5,000 years ago.

5. **Orange**: At this level, individuals begin to play their own game within society, aimed at victory and dominance. In

some sense, this level may resemble the third level, but with adherence to the fundamental rules of the fourth level. Progress is achieved through understanding and realizing the secrets of the world. The right strategy and tactics enable one to forge ahead and achieve superiority. There is a very clear self-identification, understanding of one's own path and goals. The conditions for individualism are formed, and comprehensive economic structures are established. Approximately 1,000 years ago.

6. **Green**: At this level, individuals start seeking balance in the world, engaging in close collaboration with their environment. Personal selfish goals become less of a concern. There is a need to do something for others to transform the world we live in into a better place. Liberation from greed, prejudices, and dogmatic beliefs. Self-enrichment and the enrichment of the world through spirituality, harmony, and balance. Struggle for human freedom in various manifestations, human rights, and collectivism. Approximately 150 years ago.

7. **Yellow**: Integrative level. Awareness of oneself as part of the world and as an individual entity. Recognition of previous levels of development. Perceiving life as a kaleidoscope of hierarchies and systems. The ability to interact with them effectively and achieve efficient and constructive outcomes. Tolerance towards differences existing at various levels of Spiral Dynamics. Understanding the wholeness and complexity of the world, having unrestricted access to various knowledge and traditions, and constructing a system of holistic

interconnections. Approximately 50 years ago.

8. **Turquoise**: Holistic level. Experiencing wholeness through the mind and spirituality. Understanding that human identity, on one hand, is individual, and on the other hand, is a part of a larger spiritual system. Holistic thinking is present. Globalism and the ecology of both the world and consciousness. Approximately 30 years ago.

9. **Coral**: Potentially a higher level of Spiral Dynamics, but not fully interpreted by the authors. Still in the process of emergence.

Each level of Spiral Dynamics is oriented towards either the ego or the group. This progression occurs sequentially. Ego-oriented levels include beige, red, orange, yellow, and coral. Group-oriented levels include purple, blue, green, and turquoise. In the course of personal development, individuals progress through the levels of Spiral Dynamics in a sequential manner. It is worth noting that depending on the level of Spiral Dynamics, one can understand and become aware of both the internal psychological processes occurring within a person and comprehend the nature of their behavior in the external world. This model has powerful multisystem applications in various spheres of human interaction.

Multiple Intelligences by Howard Gardner

In 1983, the American psychologist Howard Gardner presented his concept of multiple intelligences in his book "Frames of Mind." In his work, he categorized individuals into seven types based on their preferred ways of understanding the world and the dominance of a specific intellectual vector. Gardner identified the following types of intelligence: linguistic, logical-mathematical, musical, bodily-kinesthetic, spatial-visual, interpersonal, and intrapersonal. In addition to the seven primary intelligences, he also identified three additional ones: naturalistic, spiritual, and moral.

According to Howard Gardner, the different types of intelligence represent various lines of development throughout a person's life. Working with these lines can serve as an excellent diagnostic tool as well as an instrument for integrative coaching and psychotherapy. However, it is important to note that the applicability of the lines of development and multiple intelligences extends far beyond the context of psychotherapy.

Howard Gardner comments that in his research, he discovered 24 potential lines of development, which can be considered as specific types of intelligence to some extent.

List of Types of Intelligence According to Gardner

1. **Linguistic Intelligence**: Ability to easily learn different languages and understand the structure, rules, and peculiarities of language.

2. **Logical-Mathematical Intelligence**: Ability to think in a logical and mathematical manner.

3. **Musical Intelligence**: Ability to sense, create, and convey musical harmony.

4. **Bodily-Kinesthetic Intelligence**: Excellent control over

the body, fine motor skills, and overall body coordination.

5. **Spatial-Visual Intelligence**: Ability to create and manipulate visual images. Creative and artistic thinking.

6. **Interpersonal Intelligence**: Excellent communication skills, the ability to quickly establish rapport with others, and the ability to create and maintain social connections.

7. **Intrapersonal Intelligence**: Ability for self-reflection and self-awareness. Deep understanding of oneself and the world. Philosophical thinking.

8. **Naturalistic Intelligence**: Interaction with the natural environment, concern for ecology.

9. **Spiritual Intelligence**: Engagement with religion and various aspects of spiritual development.

10. **Moral Intelligence**: Ethical and moral aspects of life; advocacy for rights; jurisprudence; defense of social positions.

Spiritual States According to Ken Wilber

Wilber presents distinctions between four primary types of spiritual experiences that can be accessible to individuals:

- **Natural Mysticism**: An example of this experience can be the sense of unity with nature while walking through a forest after rain.

- **Divine Mysticism**: An example can be the experience of encountering a spiritual image during meditation.

- **Formless Mysticism**: An example can be the experience of emptiness, the abyss of consciousness. Here, one can recall Nietzsche and his phrase, "If you gaze long into an abyss, the abyss also gazes into you."

- **Non-Dual Mysticism**: An example can be a unique state of unity of opposites, interconnectedness of all living beings, and their equal value.

Cognitive Styles

The term "cognitive styles" was first mentioned by Alfred Adler to denote the characteristics of stable individual personality traits, cognitive abilities, and various investigative strategies. In Adlerian individual psychology, cognitive styles of personality were viewed as a specific form of individuality, structured by goals and various ways of achieving them.

After Adler, significant contributions to the study of cognitive styles were made by G. Allport, C. Stagner, G. Witkin, V. A. Kolga, M. A. Kholodnaya, and A. Libin.

In Neuro-Linguistic Programming (NLP), there is a concept of personality metaprograms, which are almost synonymous with the notion of cognitive styles. Some metaprograms were discussed in the chapter dedicated to NLP.

Currently, cognitive styles are understood as certain forms of cognitive dichotomies through which we filter our experiences. There is experimental evidence that cognitive styles are closely related to the intellectual sphere of personality, temperament, and motivational aspects. Typically, the literature on cognitive styles describes 10-15 types.

Let's consider some cognitive styles.

1. **Cognitive simplicity or complexity**: Some individuals have a dominant inclination to create clear and simple descriptions of the external world without excessive interpretations. Others, on the contrary, tend to have interpretations filled with excessive details.

2. **Narrow or broad range of equivalence**: Some people tend to differentiate objects in the world based on specific details inherent to them, while others do so based on generalized qualities associated with them.

3. **Impulsivity or reflectivity**: Impulsive individuals make quick and thoughtless decisions and actions, which often lead to a high number of errors. Reflective individuals, on the other hand, take much longer to ponder decisions and approach situations with deeper contemplation. Naturally, the number of life mistakes is significantly lower for reflective individuals compared to impulsive ones.

4. **Focusing or scanning control**: Individuals with focusing control fully concentrate their attention on a specific process or feature during interactions with the world and when solving tasks. As a result, they may ignore a considerable amount of various task-related details. In contrast, individuals with scanning control pay great attention to details, but maintaining complete focus on one thing can be challenging for them.

5. **Low or high tolerance for unrealistic experiences**: Tolerant individuals strive to evaluate their experiences based on their immediate characteristics, subjecting them to constructive analysis. In contrast, intolerant individuals tend to strongly resist experiences that significantly deviate from their core beliefs.

Socionic Personality Types

The term "socionics" was coined by Estonian psychologist Aushra Augustinavichute based on the typology of Carl Gustav Jung and the theory of informational metabolism by A. Kempinski. Socionics is concerned with studying the mechanisms of the psyche through which individuals perceive, filter, and evaluate various types of incoming information - verbal, nonverbal, discrete, emotional, sensory, and so on. The individual, in the context of socionics, is viewed as a specific system of informational connections that adhere to specific rules.

Augustinavichute first presented her comprehensive ideas about socionics in her book "On the Dual Nature of Man," published in 1980, which was based on her creative reinterpretation of Jung's concepts of psychotypes. Carl Jung identified four main characteristics of personality - thinking, feeling, sensing, and intuition. He believed that there were types of people who were accentuated in one or more of these characteristics. Jung also differentiated individuals into extraverts and introverts. Thus, if we construct a two-dimensional matrix, we have eight primary personality types. Furthermore, to make the descriptions of the types more accurate, Jung introduced an additional, secondary interpretation of the types. The secondary interpretation can be examined within the framework of the following matrix.

Basic Interpretation	Additional Interpretation
Thinking	Sensation
	Intuition
Feeling	Sensation
	Intuition
Sensing	Thinking
	Feeling
Intuition	Thinking
	Feeling

Variability of Personality Types

In this case, we can observe the dual division made by Jung. He interpreted thinking and feeling as rational characteristics that can intersect with sensing and intuition, which are irrational characteristics of personality. Therefore, we can see the emergence of specific combinations, as indicated in the table.

Additionally, as evident from the table, a person can have a dominant rational or irrational characteristic. In her socionics model, Augustinavičiūtė replaced the term "thinking" with "logic" and "feeling" with "ethics." She referred to the combination of the eight primary and secondary functions that Carl Jung presented as "variants of informational metabolism." She began to develop theories that these variants of informational metabolism are specific filters of consciousness that determine and influence the ways of perceiving the world and the nature of interaction with it. They also have a direct connection to a person's character.

Considering the primary function, secondary function, and extraverted or introverted reference, socionics gives rise to 16 main personality types, each possessing its own specific properties and qualities. Augustinavičiūtė believes that all 16 types form a cohesive information structure, which she named "socion."

The peculiarity of the socionics matrix of personality types lies not only in the identification of specific personality types but also in the study of their possible interaction patterns, compatibility, and incompatibility. In her book "On the Dual Nature of Man," Augustinavičiūtė presents an extensive analysis of representatives of each personality type and draws numerous analogies with various well-known historical characters. However, there is a small problem: the assignment of these characters to specific types lacks clear criteria, which undermines the objectivity and validity of her judgments.

Due to these reasons, socionics is not currently recognized as a fully established scientific discipline and is often regarded as a quasi-scientific system. Socionic tests emerged at the early stages of the discipline's development. In addition to tests for determining socionic type, other methods such as interviews, experiments, observations, dossier studies, etc., can be employed.

Despite the various contentious aspects of socionics, its typology has the potential to make an invaluable contribution to the theory and practice of understanding the diversity of psychological personality types.

No.	Primary Function	Secondary Function	Extrovert Introvert	Pseudonym
1	Logic	Sensation	Extrovert	Administrator
2			Introvert	Inspector
3		Intuition	Extrovert	Entrepreneur
4			Introvert	Analyst
5	Ethical	Sensation	Extrovert	Enthusiast
6			Introvert	Conservator
7		Intuition	Extrovert	Mentor
8			Introvert	Humanist
9	Sensation	Logic	Extrovert	Marshal
10			Introvert	Craftsman
11		Ethical	Extrovert	Politician
12			Introvert	Mediator
13	Intuition	Logic	Extrovert	Seeker
14			Introvert	Critic
15		Ethical	Extrovert	Counselor
16			Introvert	Lyricist

Expanded Matrix of Socionic Personality Types

Enneagram and Enneatypes

The concept of the Enneagram and Enneatypes was developed in the 1970s by Oscar Ichazo and Claudio Naranjo. It is worth noting that the ideas of mystic George Gurdjieff also influenced the formation of the Enneagram.

Enneagram (from the Greek words "ennéa," meaning "nine," and "grámma," meaning "written character or figure") is a model consisting of nine personality types and their interrelationships. In essence, the Enneagram model can be compared to the Socionic personality types proposed by Augustinavichiute.

The model describes nine deep unconscious drives that can exist within a person's psyche and how these drives can influence the cognitive, emotional, and behavioral aspects of human existence. They affect character manifestations, transform one's life path, and guide the processes of self-actualization. In addition to the typology itself, the Enneagram pays significant attention to the structure of potential transactions and the system of relationships between individuals belonging to different Enneatypes.

Wilts and Palmer argue that ideas similar to those of the Enneagram can be found in the works of Evagrius Ponticus, a Christian mystic who lived in Alexandria in the 4th century. In his writings, Evagrius described eight thoughts that later formed the basis of the doctrine of the seven deadly sins. He considered "self-love" as the foundational ninth thought, believing that all others follow from it. In a sense, self-love, according to Evagrius, can be seen as a metathought or the thought of thoughts, a specific unifying category. Besides describing the thoughts themselves, Evagrius outlined eight ways to combat and counteract them.

In its modern form, the Enneagram system began to be taught by Oscar Ichazo, a native of Bolivia, in the 1950s. Ichazo referred to his practice as "protoanalysis" and utilized not only the Enneagram but also other symbols and ideas. Claudio Naranjo, upon encountering Oscar Ichazo's Enneagram ideas, began teaching it in the United States in his own interpretation. Subsequently, the teaching of the Enneagram spread and gained popularity among psychotherapists and Christian clergy. Some Jesuit priests started teaching the Enneagram and considering it through the lens of Christian spirituality. However, the official Vatican did not recognize the Enneagram as a suitable tool for spiritual development. Additionally, the Enneagram has gained significant popularity in New Age circles.

One of the existing interpretations of the nine core Enneatypes is presented in the table below (the names in the table are based on the works of D. Riso, R. Hudson, and H. Makan). Each personality type is divided into three subtypes. It is believed that the subtype is directly related to the instinctual drive that dominates a person's life strategies. In the practice of the Enneagram, three primary instinctual energies are distinguished: self-preservation instinct, sexual instinct, and social instinct. Depending on which instinct dominates, different needs begin to prevail in a person.

Correspondence of Needs with Instincts

With a dominance of the self-preservation instinct, needs related to safety, health, and material well-being prevail.

With a dominance of the sexual instinct, needs related to close relationships prevail.

With a dominance of the social instinct, needs related to social recognition, status, and position in society prevail.

Although the Enneagram and the Enneatypes model have gained many supporters among practicing psychotherapists, this model is not recognized in academic circles due to the lack of valid tests that accurately determine a person's Enneatype. Moreover, within the Enneagram method itself, there are different schools of thought that may provide varying interpretations of its theoretical and practical positions. This further complicates the task of validation due to the diversity of subjective views on the subject matter.

No.	Character Role	Passion	Ego Fixation	Basic Desire	Basic Fear	Temptation	Virtue
1	Perfectionist	Anger	Resentment	To be good, ethical, balanced	To be bad, unethical, flawed	Hypocrisy, excessive criticism	Serenity
2	Helper	Pride	Flattery	To be loved	To be unloved	Neglecting one's own needs	Humility
3	Achiever	Self-deception	Vanity	To feel valuable	To have no worth	Striving to always be the best	Authenticity
4	Individualist	Envy	Melancholy (Lack)	To be authentic	To have no identity	Indulging in imagination in the quest for self-discovery	Equanimity
5	Observer	Avarice	Isolation	To be competent	To be helpless	Replacing direct experience with mental concepts	Generosity
6	Skeptic Loyalist	Fear	Doubt	To have support	To be left without support	Indecisiveness doubts	Courage
7	Enthusiast	Gluttony	Planning, deceit	To be satisfied	To experience pain and deprivation	Feeling that happiness and fulfillment are elsewhere	Sobriety
8	Challenger	Lust	Justice (Struggle)	To be protected and independent	To be controlled by others	Considering oneself completely self-sufficient	Innocence
9	Peacemaker	Sloth	Self-forgetting	To be whole	To be divided, disconnected	Avoiding conflicts	Energy (Wholeness)

Table of Enneatypes

Integral Life Practice

Ken Wilber, based on his theoretical and practical inquiries, proposed a specific type of practice that can largely be referred to as a practice of general self-development but simultaneously has, in my opinion, the most direct relation to psychotherapy.

According to Wilber, Integral Life Practice (ILP) aims to facilitate the realization of the spectrum of potentials that can be inherent in the human personality.

The essence of ILP is quite simple—it involves focusing attention and activity on twelve core dimensions. These dimensions are formed as a matrix through the combination of levels of body, mind, spirit, and shadow, as well as sectors of Self, culture, and nature. The practice consists of key foundational modules.

The "**Body**" module encompasses three fundamental aspects of working with the body, or, as Wilber puts it, the training of the three bodies. This training includes gross physical exercises such as fitness and bodybuilding, exercises with the subtle body, such as qigong and tai chi, as well as exercises for working with the causal-transcendental body, which Wilber describes as "the sense of infinity, cycles of light, and life." Working with the causal body involves certain static and dynamic meditative exercises that may incorporate specific mental work, chanting mantras, or affirmations. For example, paying homage to a

Buddha statue can be interpreted as a causal bodily exercise.

In the "**Mind**" module, we can engage in activities such as reading, studying, training intellect, memory, attention, and more.

The "**Spirit**" module may involve various forms of meditation specific to different spiritual traditions, such as prayers, chanting mantras, Zen, Kabbalah, Vipassana, and more.

In the "**Shadow**" module, attention is focused on various forms of psychotherapy, self-exploration, and the exploration of one's repressions and suppressions. Here, a wide range of psychotherapeutic forms, techniques, and practices can be employed, depending on personal preference: NLP, hypnosis and self-hypnosis, autogenic training, psychoanalysis, art therapy, and others.

Each module of Integral Life Practice offers a unique pathway for personal growth and self-realization. By engaging in practices that target the mind, spirit, and shadow, individuals can delve into different dimensions of their being and gain insight into their psychological patterns, spiritual connection, and the integration of their shadow aspects.

Body (Physical, Subtle, Causal)	Mind (Education, Intellect, Memory, Attention)	Spirit (Meditation, Prayer, Chanting of Mantras, Contemplation)	Shadow (Psychotherapy)
Fitness (Physical) Bodybuilding (Physical) Pilates (Physical) Yoga (Physical and Subtle) Qigong (Subtle) Tai Chi (Physical and Subtle) Ritualistic Body Practices (Causal)	Reading Books Watching Educational Videos Attending Seminars Intellectual Training Memory Training Attention Training	Meditation Prayer Chanting of Mantras Shamanic Contemplation Kabbalah Transcendental Meditation Kundalini Yoga	NLP (Neuro-Linguistic Programming) Hypnosis Psychoanalysis Gestalt Psychotherapy Art Therapy

Matrix of the Four Core Modules of Integral Life

In addition to the four foundational modules of ILP, Ken Wilber includes additional ones such as ethics, sexuality, work, emotions, and relationships. It is suggested that individuals choose at least one practice from each of the four foundational modules and begin engaging in them regularly.

Ken Wilber writes that if the integral AQAL model is applied as a specific guiding coordinate system for organizing and understanding a particular sphere of activity, it can be referred to as an "integral operating system" (IOS). This system allows for a significant increase in the level of effectiveness in interacting with the chosen sphere of activity by adjusting perception filters to accommodate the maximum possible diversity.

In my opinion, the application of ILP in the context of psychotherapeutic work creates new and unique opportunities and methods for utilizing a wide range of existing schools and methods of psychotherapy.

A Brief Message from the Author

Mastering complex psychotherapeutic theories and practices can be a challenging journey. By sharing your experience with this book, you can guide others who are on the same path. Your review could inspire someone to take the next step in deepening their knowledge and applying these insights to make meaningful changes in their life.

Thank you for your support and for taking the time to share your thoughts! Your feedback helps us refine our offerings and empowers others in their pursuit of mastering psychotherapy. If this book has been valuable to you, I'd be grateful if you could take a moment to leave a review. **Your positive rating would mean a lot!**

To share your feedback, simply scan the QR code or click the link below:

psychemaster.com/recommends/review-integrative-therapy

A BRIEF MESSAGE FROM THE AUTHOR

Bibliography

1. Andreas, S., Faulkner, C. NLP: New Technologies of Achievement. Kyiv: Sofia; Moscow: Helios Publishers, 2001. ISBN 5-220-00392-5.
2. Augustinavichyute, A. Socionics: Psychotypes. Tests. Compiled by L. Filippov. Moscow: AST Publishers; St. Petersburg: Terra Fantastica, 1998.
3. Byron, A. Lewis. The Magic of Neuro-Linguistic Programming Revealed. St. Petersburg: Petersburg-XXI, 1999.
4. Bandler, R., Grinder, J. The Structure of Magic. St. Petersburg: Prime-Evroznak, 2004. Volume 1: ISBN 5-93878-151-5.
5. Bandler, R., Grinder, J. The Structure of Magic. St. Petersburg: Prime-Evroznak, 2004. Volume 2: ISBN 5-93878-152-3.
6. Bandler, R., Grinder, J. Patterns of Hypnotic Techniques of Milton H. Erickson from the Perspective of NLP. Simferopol: Renome, 1999. ISBN 966-7198-31-6.
7. Bandler, R., Grinder, J. Frogs into Princes: Neuro Linguistic Programming. Moscow: Flint, 2000. ISBN 7-256-37680-9.
8. Grinder, J., Delozier, D. Turtles All the Way Down. Moscow: Prime-Evroznak, 2005. ISBN 5-93878-165-5.
9. Grinder, J., Bostic St. Claire, C. Whispering in the Wind:

The New Code of NLP. Moscow: Prime-Evroznak, 2005. ISBN 5-93878-188-4.

10. Dilts, R. Sleight of Mouth: The Magic of Conversational Belief Change. St. Petersburg: Piter, 2000.
11. O'Connor, J., Seymour, J. Introducing Neuro-Linguistic Programming. Chelyabinsk: "Library of A. Miller," 1998.
12. Wilber, K. No Boundary: Eastern and Western Approaches to Personal Growth. 1998, 2003. ISBN 5-17-018322-4.
13. Wilber, K. Atman: A Transpersonal View of Human Development. Moscow: AST Publishers, 1999, 2004. ISBN 5-17-021069-8.
14. Wilber, K. Spirit: An Integral Vision for a World Gone Slightly Mad. Moscow: AST Publishers, 2002. ISBN 5-17-014321-4.
15. Wilber, K. One Taste: The Journals of Ken Wilber. 2004. ISBN 5-17-021067-1.
16. Wilber, K. Integral Psychology: Consciousness, Spirit, Psychology, Therapy. 2004. ISBN 5-17-021067-1.
17. Wilber, K. A Brief History of Everything. Moscow: AST Publishers, 2006. ISBN 5-17-036016-9. Reprint: Moscow: Postum, 2015. - 624 p. - ISBN 978-5-91478-035-4.
18. Wilber, K. Grace and Grit. Moscow: Otkryty Mir, 2008. - 656 p. - 3000 copies. - ISBN 978-5-9743-0127-8. Reprint: Moscow: Postum, 2013. - 656 p. - 3000 copies. - ISBN 978-5-91478-025-5.
19. Wilber, K. Integral Vision. Moscow: Otkryty Mir, 2009. ISBN 978-5-9743-0156-8.
20. Wilber, K. A Theory of Everything. Moscow: Postum, 2013. ISBN 978-5-91478-027-9.
21. Wilber, K. Integral Spirituality. Electronic edition. Moscow: Ipraktik, 2013. Google Books.

22. Wilber, K. Boomeritis. Electronic edition. Moscow: Ipraktik, 2013. Google Books.
23. Wilber, K. Eye of Spirit: Flesh, Mind, and Seeing. Integral World. Moscow: "RIPOl classic," 2016.

About the Author

Dr. **Artem Kudelia**, a psychologist with a PhD and a practicing therapist, has extensive expertise in integrative approaches. He possesses comprehensive knowledge of a wide range of psychotherapeutic methods, including humanistic and existential theories, as well as the practical application of cognitive-behavioral therapy (CBT) to effectively address issues such as anxiety, depression, obsessive thoughts, compulsions, social phobias, and complex emotions. His books are valuable resources for professionals and individuals interested in managing their mental health. In addition to managing symptoms, he helps his clients toward self-actualization in various aspects of their lives, including social, career, and personal aspects.

You can connect with me on:

- https://facebook.com/psyche.masters
- https://instagram.com/psyche.masters
- https://threads.net/@psyche.masters
- https://youtube.com/@psyche.masters
- https://tiktok.com/@psyche.masters
- https://pinterest.com/psychemasters

Subscribe to my newsletter:

https://psychemaster.com/early-reader-signup

Also by Artem Kudelia PhD

The ***Psychology & Psychotherapy Theories & Practices*** series offers a detailed examination of the history, theoretical foundations, and practical applications of fundamental approaches in psychotherapy. It is an indispensable resource for psychologists, medical professionals, psychology students, and anyone interested in understanding these complex subjects.

Additionally, the ***Cognitive Behavioral Therapy Self-Help Guide: 15 Steps to Mental Health*** series provides actionable guidance for overcoming various psychological challenges, such as anxiety, depression, excessive anger, obsessive thoughts, compulsions, social phobias, health anxiety, and intricate emotional struggles. These topics were chosen because many individuals facing these challenges often lack awareness of the underlying dynamics. By gaining insight into these processes, individuals can make informed decisions about seeking help, reinforcing the idea that knowledge is a powerful tool for personal empowerment.

Together, these series offer invaluable resources for those interested in psychology, whether for academic study or personal development, by providing comprehensive insights and practical tools that contribute to improved mental well-being.

Psychotherapy Fundamentals Complete Guide

Are you struggling to understand complex psychotherapeutic theories?

Psychotherapy Fundamentals: Complete Guide simplifies the intricate world of psychotherapy, making it accessible and actionable for those interested in self-discovery, self-education, and readers with a wide range of interests.

♥ Imagine confidently navigating psychotherapeutic real-world scenarios with ease.

This book is your *comprehensive roadmap to achieving a deep and practical understanding of psychotherapy*. You'll learn to simplify complex theories and integrate them effectively into your life and practice.

Gain a comprehensive understanding of various therapeutic approaches, including *provocative* therapy, *humanistic* therapy, *somatic* therapy, *existential* therapy, *drama* therapy, *psychedelic* and *post-psychedelic* therapy, *anti-psychiatric* therapy, and *integrative* therapy. Each chapter delves into the key themes and methods of these psychotherapy modalities, broadening the horizons for those interested in self-discovery, self-education, and lifelong learning.

▼

https://books2read.com/Psychotherapy-Fundamentals

Hypnotherapy Fundamentals
Complete Guide

Are you ready to uncover the secrets of hypnotherapy?

This comprehensive guide immerses you in the ***theory*** *and history of hypnosis*, providing a solid foundation for understanding the principles underlying hypnotherapy.

Explore the various techniques and approaches used in *hypnotherapy* ***training*** through ***practice exercises***, including the art of *suggestion* and deepening *hypnotic trance states*, the creation of therapeutic propositions, and the utilization of the power of the subconscious mind.

Learn how to effectively apply *hypnotherapy techniques* to address a wide range of issues, from managing stress and anxiety to overcoming phobias and habits.

Gain an understanding of the transformative potential of hypnosis and its applications for personal growth and well-being.

Unlock the secrets of harnessing the power of the mind and creating positive changes in yourself and others.

https://books2read.com/Hypnotherapy-Fundamentals

Psychology of Love & Death
Therapeutic Path to Fundamental Balance in Life and Relationships

How to Achieve Fundamental Balance in Life and Relationships?

Explore dualistic nature of human consciousness, along with the profound impact of seeking balance between fundamental continuums of *love and death, instinct and spirituality, masculinity and femininity* in shaping our experiences and relationships.

Explore the psychopathological profiles and manifestations of love and death, including profiles such as hysteria, paranoia, psychopathy, and others.

Uncover different types of love, from eros to agape, and study the *three-component Theory of Love.*

Familiarize yourself with *real-life psychotherapy cases* that illustrate the complexities of love, death, and therapy and gain *valuable insights* into the human experience and its challenges.

▼

https://books2read.com/Psychology-of-Love-and-Death

Breathwork Therapy Seminar Holotropic Journey to Unconscious Mind Secrets

Tap Into the Wisdom of Transpersonal Psychology!

This book is the transcript of a seminar that addresses the profound questions of *subconsciousness*, offering a unique perspective on personal growth and healing.

Gain profound insights into the workings of your mind and explore the mysteries of human consciousness.

Access practical exercises and *techniques* to facilitate personal growth, healing, and self-awareness through *breathwork*.

Written for seekers of self-awareness, psychology enthusiasts, and anyone curious about the depths of the human mind.

Explore the integration of spirituality and psychology, uncovering your inner potential.

▼

https://books2read.com/Breathwork-Therapy

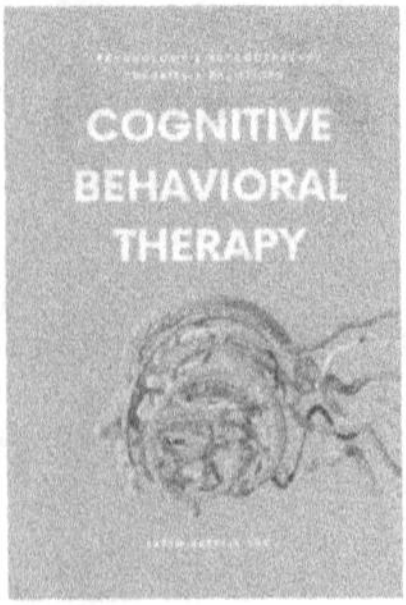

Cognitive Behavioral Therapy
Managing Anxiety and Depression

Explore the roots of anxiety and learn why it's a fundamental aspect of the human experience.

An in-depth exploration of *Panic Disorder*, addressing the irrational fears associated with it.

Examine the nuances of *Social Anxiety* and its impact on personal and professional spheres.

Dive into the world of *Obsessive-Compulsive Disorder*, unraveling its complexities.

Understand the genetic predispositions and learn effective strategies to manage obsessions and compulsions.

Explore *PTSD* from its roots to its biological manifestations. Delve into the trauma cycles, and discover therapeutic techniques for stabilization and overcoming trauma.

Grasp the degrees of *Depression*, from mild to severe, debunking common myths.

▼

https://books2read.com/Cognitive-Behavioral-Therapy

Psychotherapy
Introduction to Healing Vectors

Do you want to understand the variety of methods of psychotherapy and choose the one that is best for you?

In the vast world of psycho-technologies, there are numerous methods of psychotherapy that encompass a wide range of *personality theories* and concepts.

Drawing upon an integral framework, the book maps out the complex *landscape of psychotherapy*, encompassing vectors such as *psychoanalytic*, *hypnotic*, *provocative*, *humanistic*, *behavioral*, *existential*, *transpersonal*, *cognitive*, *somatic*, *psychodramatic* and *psychedelic* therapies, among many others.

This book will provide you with valuable knowledge that will allow you to choose the most suitable therapeutic path for specific circumstances and personality types.

https://books2read.com/Psychotherapy-Introduction

Provocative Therapy
The Healing Power of Dark Humor

Who said that psychotherapy can't be hilariously funny?

Explore innovative ideas about the power of humor in psychotherapy and coaching.

Uncover the archetypal foundation of Provocative Therapy inspired by the myths of the Trickster and the Holy Fool.

Delve into the transformational potential of *Group Provocative Psychotherapy* and the important rules that define successful group dynamics.

Explore the effectiveness of *Provocative Coaching* and its focus points.

Dive into the fascinating world of *Provocative Drama* and its role in therapeutic interventions.

Explore the *pathopsychological profiles*, including *hysteroid, paranoid, psychopathic, obsessive-compulsive, schizoid, epileptoid, schizophrenic*, and *manic-depressive* profiles.

▼

https://books2read.com/Provocative-Therapy

Humanistic Therapy
From Crisis to Self-Actualization

Do you want to explore a world where people are seen as unique holistic systems with infinite potential waiting to be discovered?

Immerse yourself in the theories and practices of humanistic therapy and explore the *transformative path from crisis to self-actualization.*

Unlike psychoanalysis, which focuses on internal complexes and personal traumas, humanistic therapy emphasizes the *study and development of positive personality qualities.*

Humanistic philosophy has also influenced fields such as *education*, promoting *empathy* and *support* as the foundation of learning.

This holistic approach recognizes the *interconnectedness of mind, body, and spirit* and seeks to stimulate personal *growth* and *well-being.*

Take the first step towards self-awareness, personal growth, and a more fulfilling existence.

▼

https://books2read.com/Humanistic-Therapy

Somatic Therapy
The Wisdom of the Body

Would you like to establish a connection with your body and access the source of wisdom?

Unleash the transformative power of *somatic therapy* and embark on a journey of *self-discovery* and *healing.*

Explore the profound connection between the *mind and body.*

Discover the *seven levels of muscular armor* and their connection to specific emotions such as sadness, anger, and fear.

By exploring different body segments, you will unlock *powerful techniques* for releasing pent-up emotions and promoting harmony throughout the organism. From *eye movements* and *jaw exercises* to *deep breathing* and *body movements*, this book offers *practical methods* for *accessing the wisdom of the body* and *restoring emotional balance.*

Acquire unique knowledge about *healing after birth trauma and psychosomatic medicine.*

https://books2read.com/Somatic-Therapy

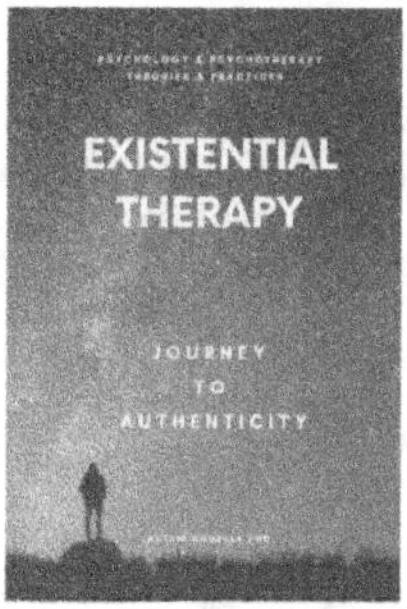

Existential Therapy
Journey to Authenticity

Do you want to know who you really are? What is your personal meaning of existence?

Embark on a *transformative journey* to uncover your *true essence* and embrace the *principles* of existential therapy.

Explore the rich philosophical roots of *existential psychotherapy* and find your path to *personal authenticity.*

Explore key themes such as *freedom, responsibility, meaning,* and *choice*, and learn to courageously and authentically navigate the complexities of existence.

This book provides *practical ideas and techniques* for *applying the principles of existential therapy* to your own life.

Gain a deep *understanding* of your *values, beliefs*, and *desires*, and learn to *embrace uncertainty* and *transform* life's *challenges* into *opportunities* for *growth* and *self-discovery.*

https://books2read.com/Existential-Therapy

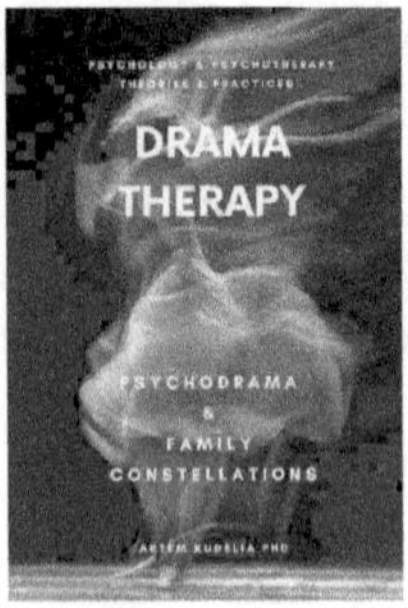

Drama Therapy
Potential of Psychodrama and Family Constellations

Explore the unique world of drama therapeutic approach!

Therapeutic model of intervention that encompasses 12 *powerful speech patterns* capable of significantly *influencing conscious and unconscious processes.*

Through *psychodramatic techniques* and *family constellations*, you will *gain practical knowledge* to enhance your therapeutic practice.

Addressing a wide spectrum of *psychopathological profiles*, including *hysteria, paranoia*, and *obsessive-compulsive disorders*, this book equips you with effective dramatherapeutic activities and psychodynamic exercises.

It serves as a *comprehensive guide* to *crisis intervention, counseling theory*, and *strategies for addiction rehabilitation.*

Gain an understanding of the right hemisphere and the *neuroscience* underlying drama therapy, and learn to *navigate complex emotional situations* with *understanding* and *acceptance.*

▼

https://books2read.com/Drama-Therapy-Constellations

Psychedelic Therapy
The Healing Power Therapeutic Journeys

Embark on a transformative journey into the world of psychedelic therapy!

Explore the fascinating *history* of *psychedelic substances* and potential benefits of working with consciousness-altering substances in clinical practice.

Learn comprehensive information on various *psychedelic therapies*, including *ketamine therapy*, *psilocybin*-assisted psychotherapy, *MDMA*-assisted psychotherapy, and *ibogaine* psychotherapy.

Gain knowledge about *mental health* in the *perinatal period*, the *role of hypnosis*, and the transformative power of *holotropic breathwork.*

Understand the profound impact of *psychedelic medicine* and the potential of *psilocybin microdosing.*

Explore the therapeutic applications of *ketamine* in the *treatment of depression* and *psychosynthesis in coaching.*

▼

https://books2read.com/Psychedelic-Therapy-Journey

Beyond Psychiatry
Exploring Anti-Psychiatry Method

Challenge traditional psychiatry and psychotherapy!

This book presents an *alternative to conventional* ideas of normalcy and offers a *fresh perspective on psychological disorders*, inviting readers to question existing paradigms.

Delve deeper into *psychopathological profiles* and *anti-psychiatric* forms of psychotherapy, examining various profiles including *hysteria, paranoia, psychopathy*, and more.

Gain an understanding of the intersection of psychotherapy and existential philosophy, *challenging the myth of mental illness* within families.

Explore the *treatment of psychosis, trauma*, and *emotional disorders from a holistic perspective.*

▼

https://books2read.com/Beyond-Psychiatry

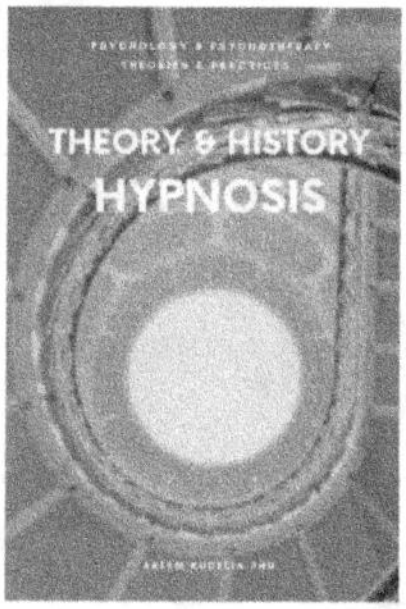

Theory & History of Hypnosis
Exploring Altered State of Mind in Trance

Immerse yourself in the fascinating world of hypnosis and explore the history and theory of altered states of consciousness!

This book sheds light on *historical trance practices* and the *role of shamanism*, tracing its influence on *modern psychospiritual orientations.*

Discover the benefits of this book by exploring the *history of trance practices and hypnotherapy.*

Explore the *evolution* of *shamanism*, its connection to *religion*, and its pre-religious *philosophy*, which offered deep insights into the structure of the universe and the mysteries of the spiritual world.

Discover various *hypnotic phenomena* and *states of consciousness* that can be induced in a trance state.

Explore their potential applications in *psychotherapeutic practice*, from *pain management* to the *treatment of depression.*

Learn techniques such as *self-hypnosis, deep trance induction*, and *guided healing visualizations.*

▼

https://books2read.com/Theory-and-History-of-Hypnosis

Hypnotherapy Training
A Guide for Practicing Hypnotherapists

Uncover the secrets of hypnotherapy and improve your practical hypnosis skills!

This book explores *techniques* and *practical skills* for hypnotherapists.

Dive into the depths of the *subconscious* and discover the *transformative potential* of hypnotherapy.

Discover the benefits of this book, which delves into key topics and approaches in *hypnotherapy training.*

Explore developed techniques, including rapport-building practices and the use of matching postures, movements, and breathing with the client.

Engage in exercises that enable the attainment of different trance levels and explore the motives of trance and their application in psychotherapy.

Gain an understanding of different styles and orientations of hypnotic work, from hypnoanalytic and suggestive to behavioral and transpersonal.

https://books2read.com/Hypnotherapy-Training

Healing Anxiety and Overthinking
Proven CBT Strategies for Lasting Relief

Are you exhausted from the relentless cycle of anxiety and overthinking?

Discover the 15-step program that will transform your mental health and bring peace of mind.

Millions of adults struggle with anxiety and overthinking, feeling trapped in a cycle of worry and stress. But it doesn't have to be this way. "*Healing Anxiety and Overthinking: Proven CBT Strategies for Lasting Relief*" offers a comprehensive guide to breaking free from the grip of anxiety using practical, proven **Cognitive Behavioral Therapy** (**CBT**) strategies.

❤ ***Imagine waking up every day with a clear mind, free from the constant barrage of anxious thoughts***

This book is your roadmap to achieving that transformation in just 15 steps. You'll learn to understand the nature of your anxiety, identify its triggers, and apply effective techniques to manage and overcome it.

Take Control of Your Mental Health

Don't let anxiety and overthinking rule your life. With "*Healing Anxiety and Overthinking*," you'll gain the tools and confidence to achieve peace of mind and live the life you deserve.

Mastering Intrusive Thoughts
Practical CBT Techniques for Managing OCD

Is ***OCD*** *ruling your life with intrusive thoughts and compulsions?*

Take back control with scientifically-proven CBT techniques designed to help you regain peace of mind.

Millions of adults struggle with obsessive-compulsive disorder (OCD), caught in a relentless cycle of intrusive thoughts and compulsive behaviors. "Mastering Intrusive Thoughts" is your step-by-step guide to breaking free from the grip of OCD using practical, evidence-based Cognitive Behavioral Therapy (CBT) techniques.

❤ Picture yourself waking up with a calm, focused mind, no longer burdened by the constant anxiety of unwanted thoughts.

In this book, Dr. Artem Kudelia offers a clear and actionable path to mastering your thoughts in 15 manageable steps. Whether you're new to CBT or have tried other methods without success, this guide provides the tools you need to finally achieve relief.

✔ Take the First Step Towards Mental Freedom

You'll gain the knowledge and confidence to conquer your **OCD** and reclaim your peace of mind.

The Anger Solution
A CBT Program for Emotional Balance

Are you tired of living with persistent anger and overwhelming stress?

Discover a practical, 15-step program designed to bring lasting peace and transform your emotional health.

Millions of adults struggle with anger and stress, feeling trapped in a cycle of frustration and tension. But it doesn't have to be this way. "The Anger Solution" offers a comprehensive guide to breaking free from the grip of anger using practical, proven Cognitive Behavioral Therapy (CBT) strategies.

❤ ***Imagine waking up every day with a calm mind, free from the constant barrage of anger and stress.***

This book is your roadmap to achieving that transformation. With clear, actionable steps, you'll learn to understand the nature of your anger, identify its triggers, and apply effective techniques to manage and overcome it.

✔ **Take Control of Your Emotional Health**

With "The Anger Solution," you'll gain the tools and confidence to achieve emotional balance and live the life you deserve.

Health Anxiety Mastery
30 Proven CBT Steps to Peace of Mind

Is health anxiety controlling your life with constant worry and fear?

Regain peace of mind with proven CBT techniques designed to help you overcome health-related anxiety and reclaim control.

Millions of people struggle with health anxiety, trapped in a cycle of physical symptoms, endless reassurance-seeking, and intrusive thoughts about their well-being. *"Health Anxiety Mastery"* offers a clear, step-by-step approach to breaking free from these patterns using practical, evidence-based Cognitive Behavioral Therapy (CBT) techniques.

♥ Imagine waking up each day calm and confident, no longer overwhelmed by fear and obsessive thoughts about your health.

In this book, you'll find 30 actionable steps to help you reduce anxiety, challenge limiting beliefs, and develop healthier thought patterns. Whether you're just beginning your journey or have tried other approaches without success, these practical tools will guide you toward lasting relief.

✔ Start Your Journey to Balanced Mental Health

How to Get Over Social Anxiety
CBT Strategies for True Confidence and Deep Connection

What if 15 proven steps could free you from social anxiety and help you connect?

Uncover a 15-step CBT program to overcome fear, stop avoidance, and build true self-confidence. Millions struggle with social anxiety, but you don't have to face it alone. This guide provides a clear, evidence-based path to transforming your social life and connecting authentically.

♥ **Imagine engaging in conversations fearlessly and forming genuine relationships free from judgment or rejection.**

With insights from proven cognitive-behavioral techniques and relatable examples, this book offers the practical tools and encouragement needed to face your fears and succeed socially.

✔ **Begin Your Journey to Confidence**

Start transforming fear into connection and reclaim control of your social life with "*How to Get Over Social Anxiety*."

Discover More by Artem Kudelia

Scan the QR code or click the link to access his author page and full collection. Each book provides detailed insights and practical guidance, exemplifying his contributions to psychology and psychotherapy.

books2read.com/Artem-Kudelia-PhD

www.ingramcontent.com/pod-product-compliance
Lightning Source LLC
LaVergne TN
LVHW022226200926
848481LV00006B/2133